# GOSPEL BEHIND BARS

*Also by Phil Shirley*

Miracles *Can* Happen

# Gospel Behind Bars

True life stories of crime and repentance

Phil Shirley

N. LONSDALE
UNITED CHURCH
LIBRARY

# Hodder & Stoughton

LONDON  SYDNEY  AUCKLAND

Copyright © 1997 by Phil Shirley

First published in Great Britain 1997

The right of Phil Shirley to be identified as the Author
of the Work has been asserted by him in accordance with the
Copyright, Designs and Patents Act 1988.

1 3 5 7 9 10 8 6 4 2

All rights reserved. No part of this publication may be
reproduced, stored in a retrieval system, or transmitted,
in any form or by any means without the prior written
permission of the publisher, nor be otherwise circulated
in any form of binding or cover other than that in which
it is published and without a similar condition being
imposed on the subsequent purchaser.

British Library Cataloguing in Publication Data
A record for this book is available from the British Library

ISBN 0 340 65625 5

Typeset by Avon Dataset Ltd, Bidford-on-Avon, Warks

Printed and bound in Great Britain by
Caledonian International Book Manufacturing Ltd, Glasgow

Hodder and Stoughton Ltd
A division of Hodder Headline PLC
338 Euston Road
London NW1 3BH

> Bring my soul out of prison,
> that I may praise thy name:
> the righteous shall compass me
> about; for thou shalt deal
> bountifully with me.
>
> Psalms 143:7

Some names have been changed to protect the innocent.

# Contents

| | | |
|---|---|---|
| | Introduction | ix |
| 1 | Black Mercury | 1 |
| 2 | Madman | 7 |
| 3 | Lost and found | 17 |
| 4 | Man in black | 21 |
| 5 | Soul-hole | 27 |
| 6 | Shark-eyes | 31 |
| 7 | The Pig | 37 |
| 8 | Reality | 45 |
| 9 | Dead man walking | 49 |
| 10 | Feel the sun | 55 |
| 11 | Blood-release | 63 |
| 12 | Paper and fire | 67 |
| 13 | Something to remind you | 71 |
| 14 | View from above | 79 |
| 15 | Still life talking | 87 |
| 16 | Back for good | 95 |
| 17 | It don't lie | 99 |
| 18 | In the end | 103 |
| 19 | Prophecy | 107 |
| 20 | Bitterness rising | 109 |

# Introduction

I was told not to write this book. In fact I was warned not to write this book, such was the cynicism and suspicion of the prison warder whom I first approached to begin my research. 'Don't do it, it's a waste of bloody time,' he insisted. 'I've met many, many people who have found God in prison and usually God lasts as long as the sentence. As soon as they get out it's "to hell with God" and back to whatever they were doing before they got nicked.'

The warder in question, whom I won't name, is retired now. He was in charge of one the largest high-security prisons in England and during his time in 'the system' met thousands and thousands of inmates. 'Many claimed to have "found God", he added, 'but I can't recall one who stuck with it. If you want my advice, and it's good advice, write about something else.'

Obviously I didn't take his advice, and I'm glad. But I've got to level with you, a lot of what he said is true. It's a fact, and I found out the hard way, like the time I tracked down the ex-con who was converted to Christianity during a seven-year stretch and joined a Christian support team who were raising funds to send a missionary to Africa.

'Can I speak to Mr X?' I asked the team secretary. 'Oh I'm afraid that won't be possible,' came the reply. 'He was arrested yesterday, for robbery.'

And there were many, many others who, as the warder warned, obviously said 'to hell the God' and returned to a life of crime. I was beginning to wonder if he was right. 'Maybe it is a waste of time,' I thought, and then there was the other big doubt – the 'victim factor'. How to justify raving about some person who murdered, raped, or did some other bad thing before 'finding God' in the nick and becoming a better person when somewhere out there is someone who is still hurting beyond belief because of what the convicted con did. It was a tough one.

Again I found out the hard way. I went to a church to talk to a vicar about a man serving ten years for the rape of a nine-year-old girl. The vicar visited this man every month and told me that several years ago the man had committed his life to God and was now a 'born-again' Christian who deeply regretted what he had done to that innocent girl. I believed the vicar and later found out that the convicted rapist really had changed. His was a genuine testimony. 'Good,' I thought, 'there is hope after all.'

But several weeks later I met the father of the young girl. It was a chance meeting. He lived close to the church where I first spoke to the vicar. Someone had obviously told him about the book. 'Are you the one who's been asking about that bastard who raped my daughter?' he said, 'because if you are you should see her first, before you

# INTRODUCTION

start gushing about God and prisons and all that rubbish. She's a zombie, a bloody zombie. She hasn't got a life any more, wakes up screaming from nightmares and wets the bed. Don't talk to me about religion and repentance. The bastard deserves to rot in hell.'

What could I say? He and all the other innocent victims hurt by the people in this book have a right to be angry. There was no way I could have justified telling the father of that young girl to forgive and forget because the 'bastard' who raped his daughter is a good guy now. It doesn't work like that. There are some things you can't forget or forgive. As Christian men and women we are supposed to forgive as God forgives those who sin against us. But we are not God. We are human, flesh and blood, and no matter how good a bad person becomes, the consequences of some crimes are so awful they cannot be reversed or erased. In God there is a way to escape from the past, but it's not an easy way or for the faint-hearted.

Fortunately, there are those who make it. People who were once evil, just plain bad, confused, reckless, stupid, or crazy, but who found a way back into the heart of God where we all belong. There is forgiveness. There is a second chance, a third, fourth, fifth chance . . . There is hope. It's not a con or an excuse. It's the reason why Jesus Christ died on the cross.

There is some truth in the words of the prison warder who told me I would be wasting my time writing this book. Some people use God just as they use other people . . . but many others find God and another way of life and never ever look back. It happens, to the worst of us, thank God.

# 1

# Black Mercury

❦

*Ray Paul, Death Row, Huntsville, Texas, USA*

In 1967 Ray Paul worked at a gas station in a small town west of Dallas, Texas. He was thirty-nine and drove a black Mercury. It had a big dent in the front wing and blood stains on the back seat. Ray was an evil man.

He raped and murdered a young girl and hid the body in the trunk of his black Mercury until the flesh started to rot. It was summertime and the heat made the stench unbearable. Ray couldn't stand it any longer, so he drove to the edge of town and dumped the decaying corpse in a pond.

The water was stagnant and covered in a thick green crust. It was also shallow and did not completely cover the body. Instead the dead girl's head and shoulders protruded from the putrid slime. Ray laughed because he thought she looked 'kinda funny', and he threw rocks at the head, clapping his hands together every time he hit the target.

Some distance away a highway patrolman stood and looked at the empty black Mercury. He noticed the big dent in the front wing and the bloodstains on the back seats. He also noticed the smell. He heard noises coming from below the highway and followed the sound until he came to the edge of the pool.

Ray Paul was waist deep in green slime trying to hide the corpse.

The highway patrolman pulled out his gun and fired a single shot into the cloudless sky. Ray Stone came quietly.

There was a time when Ray thought about changing, before it was too late. 'One day God will turn his back on you Raymond,' his mother used to say. 'He loves the sinner and hates the sin, but when the sinner keeps on sinning the gift of redemption is taken away. You heed my warning, Raymond, change your ways now, or else.'

Ray was thirteen and the skin on his back was raw from the lashes of his father's horse-whip. His father was a preacher who used to take great delight in whipping his only son. 'Take your shirt off and beg for the Lord's mercy,' he'd say, and then secretly ejaculate as he rained blows upon the boy.

The child was whipped from the age of six. In the beginning the beatings were not bad, but as he got older the ferocity increased and he often didn't deserve to be punished at all. He wasn't a bully, and his thieving was restricted to apples from a neighbour's tree.

But one night Ray woke from a fitful sleep to hear his mother's muffled screams and the sound of flesh slapping flesh and leather smacking skin.

He watched through a crack in the bedroom door as his father sodomised and whipped his wife. The next day Ray took his father's whip and attacked the girl from next door, forcing her to strip naked while he masturbated with one hand and whipped with the other.

His next six months were spent in juvenile detention, but when he came out he killed his father by fixing the brakes of his car. Early one morning the brakes failed and the car swerved off the road at the edge of town, gathering speed. It must have been doing fifty or more when it hit a canyon wall and burst into flames. The coroner said it was an accident.

The blood seeping from the wounds in Christ's hands and feet was bright red. Ray stared at the picture of the crucifixion on the prison chapel wall. The picture was old and faded but the red paint was not. He wondered why and thought that in real life the colour of blood was much darker, and for a moment he closed his tired eyes and saw crimson rivers of blood and distorted faces drowning in pain within the dark recesses of his mind.

Ray was a prisoner now, awaiting execution, and yet as he contemplated the agony of Christ on the cross he sensed freedom, not from the cold grey stone walls around him or the hands of fate in the shape of the electric chair, but freedom from the prison of his own soul.

He wanted to reach out and touch Christ but he was handcuffed to the chair in which he sat, a gaunt figure of a man with shackled ankles and tears that dripped and wet the leather of his prison issue boots.

During the weeks leading to his execution Ray attended all the prison services. Convinced of God's presence he confessed to a lifetime of evil and asked for forgiveness. It was the first time he had felt or shown remorse since the day he took his father's whip and attacked the young girl.

In the seven days leading to the morning when a room full of people watched Ray die, the man who had murdered his father and brutally raped and killed an innocent young girl wrote a letter to his ailing mother.

Mary Paul believed her son was responsible for the death of her husband but she never said anything to anyone. Now she wept for the first time since the preacher beat and raped her and the blue ink of Ray's handwriting smudged as the tears stained the paper.

'Ma, I'm sorry. I wish you were with me now because I'm scared. I'm going to die soon, I know I deserve to die but holding your hand would make me feel better.' Mary Paul's frail hands trembled as she held the letter. 'I wish now I had listened to you. I wish I had not been so bad.

'But you are wrong about God. He can forgive a sinner like me. I have seen the nails in Christ's hands and feet and have felt inside me the agony he must have endured as he hung on the cross.

'Ma I know now that he had hung there and died for me. I asked God to forgive me for all the bad things I had done and I felt all of my sins being lifted out of my body. Now as I write this letter to the one person I have only ever loved, I am left with a feeling of peace and I cried for joy all night last night.

'Even now I am overwhelmed by the love of Christ and the presence of the Holy Spirit. I wish I could live my life over again and change the things I have done but it's too late and I guess this is the only way it can end for me. Please forgive me Ma. God has.'

# 2

# Madman

*Chris Lambrianou, Parkhurst, Isle of Wight, England*

Chris lay still, his head on his arms, his face in the gutter. He felt warm and sticky from the bleeding. Each time he heard the shouts he expected another punch or another kick. They were swearing at him and spitting. Then he heard a police siren wail. It was a short distance away and suddenly they were gone. The clatter of their boots and shoes echoed down the streets. Some men picked Chris up and started to run with him away from the sound of the siren through a passageway and into a park. They laid him on a bench. One man took out a handkerchief and gave it to Chris. The others stood around and watched him wipe blood from his nose and mouth. 'They jumped me,' he said, 'but I got two of them, bust their faces right open. Bet I was the best second they ever had.' Chris laughed and the others laughed with him. 'Anyone fancy a beer.'

It is said, and with some authority, that after seven years anybody in a long-term prison must be crazy. Chris was out of his head with madness before he started the sixth year of his life sentence for murder and after seven he could hear voices inside his head saying 'kill yourself'.

He might have done so had it not been for divine intervention, which pulled him back from the edge of insanity one awful night when he fought and won a desperate battle for his soul, a soul tortured by the past and without hope for the future.

As a young man Chris did not care about the future. He lived for the moment and as long as he'd got money and respect he was happy. He loved the feel of what was happening around him. It was the 1960s, a time when everything began to explode, and Chris had a time-bomb ticking away inside him.

He was pumped with adrenaline: a predator, suited and booted and thriving in a violent world where you had to hurt them before they hurt you to survive. It was a jungle and Chris loved the thrill of it all.

Make no mistake about it, he was out for the kill. Fists, sticks, knives, and guns, whatever it took to stay on top of the game, Chris would do it, no hesitation. There were no nice guys, only winners and losers and the words defeat and fear were not in Chris's vocabulary.

'Chris did not see any danger,' a close friend recalled. 'To put it crudely, he didn't give a shit about anyone or anything. He was a lethal man, a raving lunatic. He'd do anything to make a name for himself and earn money. Burglary, wage snatches, safe blowing, protection money, pornography, he did the lot and spent his early years in and out of borstal, remand homes, and prison. He hurt quite a few people.'

Born and raised in the East End of London, Chris formed a relationship with the Kray twins, Ronald and Reginald. They liked him and although Chris was never part of their 'firm' and knew them only socially, the fact that the three were often seen sharing a drink and a joke earned Chris respect on the street.

He was made. A top gangster, at least that's what the papers said when Chris was arrested for murder shortly after the Kray twins' empire of crime collapsed toward the end of the 1960s.

Ronnie and Reggie were among nineteen men arrested in a series of dawn swoops by Scotland Yard on Thursday 9 May 1968. A couple of months later the police came for Chris and arrested him for murder. 'I was guilty as hell to accessory after the fact,' he now admits, 'but I had not murdered anybody. I was innocent of that charge.

'On the night in question I had been out with my brother and a few friends and ended up at a club. It was a private party and we were all invited. But as soon as we walked in I realised there was no party. We had walked into a trap. Reggie Kray jumped up and put a gun to another man's head.

'I could not believe it because the other guy was a friend of Reggie and Ronnie. I had seen the three of them the previous week being good friends.

'It made me quite upset and I told a friend that I did not like what was happening. Then Ronnie Kray jumped up and came over to us and asked, "What's the problem? What's the matter with him?" My friend explained that I did not like Reggie's behaviour and Ronnie snapped back, "Take him home, now."

'So I went home but did not stay there. I was worried about my brother. I got my gun and went back to the party. When I arrived the man who Reggie had threatened with the gun was already dead and in the moment of madness that I would live to regret I got myself involved in removing the body.'

Chris was sentenced at the Old Bailey with nine other men, all of whom were allegedly involved in the murder. He got life and the judge recommended fifteen years without parole.

Chris was secretly devastated but he put on a brave face. He was determined to go down with dignity and respect and as they escorted him out of court he waved to a packed gallery and said: 'See you later.'

'Unlike many gangsters Chris was intelligent as well as being a violent thug,' said the prison warder who remembers seeing Chris arrive in a category A van flanked by an armed guard. 'We knew we were getting a big fish, someone who was respected in the criminal underworld. Chris was physically a big man and also mentally very strong and clever.

'He was in the top ten most dangerous men in the system at that particular time. He was regarded as a person who was extremely dangerous and possessed a great deal of ability with regard to potential escape.'

Nothing could have been farther from Chris's

# MADMAN

mind. He was determined to bide his time. He was one of the top men in the prison and the fact that other inmates were literally falling over themselves to be his friend made his sentence slightly more tolerable. The warder was right about one thing: Chris was mentally strong and if anyone could survive a fifteen-year stretch he could.

But less than half-way through his sentence, something started to happen to Chris. He began to crack under the pressure. He'd been locked up many times but never for so long. This time the prison regime was killing him. He couldn't sleep and the stress began to take its toll mentally and physically.

'If you have an animal in a cage and you poke it long enough it's going to react,' he said, 'and I leaked out all over the place and got very angry. I was exploding and at times I was out of my head with madness.

'It all came to a head one night as I sat in my cell smoking a fag. I was not in a depressive frame of mind, but somebody started to play a record in the cell below me and whoever it was kept on playing it over and over again. It was a song by Bob Dylan called *Knocking on Heaven's Door*.

'I felt this cloud, not depression, almost intensively evil, pass over me. I became very, very angry and started pacing up and down. The music continued to play and it was all hitting me quite profoundly.'

Chris stopped suddenly and turned to look in the mirror. What he saw put the fear of God into him. The face he saw was not his own. Staring back at him was the face of an evil monster, a demon. It was the devil of his own making and for the first time in his life he realised what he had become. 'All at once I was confronted by all the badness in me,' he recalled.

'I knew right there and then that I was the evil thing in my life. I had created my own personal hell and I could see it through the reflection of my own eyes.'

It was three in the morning and Chris was still pacing up and down in his cell. Blood was running hot in his veins one minute and then as cold as ice the next. He felt like a bomb ready to explode. 'If anyone would have walked through the door of my cell at that moment I would certainly have killed them,' he said, 'I was having a real battle with evil and there was a voice inside my head saying, "Kill yourself, you're never going to get out. You are going to die here so get it over with. Kill yourself." '

In one last desperate attempt to ease his pain Chris shouted: 'Stop. I can't think like this, I've got to do something.' And he dropped to his knees and took hold of a box of books he kept under his bed. He started frantically going through the contents of the box, picking up the books and throwing them out, looking for something, anything to help him.

'There were books on philosophy, psychology, thrillers, sport, all sorts of titles,' he said, 'but then I came across a Bible. I stopped for a moment and looked at it, but threw it across the room. "It's no use to me," I thought. The only time I'd ever picked up a Bible before was when I was in a punishment cell

# MADMAN

and needed the pages to roll a fag. That's how much I thought of the Bible.

'But I was desperate and after going through all the other books again I came back to the Bible and started to read it. Immediately I knew there was something special about it. The stories I was reading were full of men of real character and strength, hard men who would die for the Christian belief. It had a profound impact on me.'

So Chris put the Bible under his pillow hoping that it would help him to get to sleep. It was now four thirty and he was exhausted. But he still could not sleep. He took the Bible and held it close to his chest and rocked himself like a baby and eventually fell asleep.

In the space of a few hours Chris had experienced a breakdown and a breakthrough. The next day felt strangely different. He could not put his finger on exactly why he felt different but he was calm and there was a peace in his soul which he had never felt before. 'During the days and weeks that followed I read the Bible and prayed. I knew I had found something more powerful than the destructive forces in my own life.

'The Bible and the message in it had given me a foothold to a better life, something I could hang on to. I had nothing else. This new-found belief offered me another perception, another angle on life and a doorway into another world which was more understanding and more compassionate.

'I was ridiculed by other inmates. The same men

who used to respect me. But I didn't care. I had found faith in God and he was giving me my life back, little by little, piece by piece and it felt good.'

Chris studied the Bible and attended services at the prison chapel during the remainder of his fifteen-year sentence. After his release he did any job which was legal, got married and had five children. They settled in a picturesque country village near Oxford but sadly the marriage was not to last.

A life of crime and many years in prison had not prepared Chris for being a sensitive husband; in the end the financial and emotional pressures became too much to bear and what had become a volatile marriage ended in divorce.

'It was hard to accept,' Chris now admits. 'I loved my wife and was devoted to my children. I still am and see them every other week. They and God are the most important things in my life, and always will be. I guess the divorce was a consequence of my past. At times I found it hard to adjust, even though in God I was a completely different man, a better person.

'I believe that the Son of God came down to earth and died for me because this world was a sinful world. I believe that Christ came to show us another way, a way of compassion, trust, and love, a way back into the heart of God where we belong.

'I was such a small mean creature but inside of me was a giant, a giant in God. This world does not understand it. You don't find God until you are on your knees. People still mock me but if what I believe is a con, what a wonderful con it is. It's got me through my life, it's marvellous, and you can keep on conning me.

'The truth is we are all playing truant but some of us have come back and said sorry. It doesn't make us perfect. We still make mistakes. We mess up but we know God is there.

'What do I want to tell my children? I'm a wonderful criminal, I'm successful so go forth and do the same? No. That is not what I want for my kids. I don't want the disappointment, the misery, deception and pain. I want them to know what love is, what honesty is, and who Jesus is. It's the only way. The other way leads to heartache. I know. I've been there.'

Chris is now working as a counsellor for young offenders at a drug rehabilitation centre near Oxford. He calls it 'the last stop hotel between here and hell'.

# 3

# Lost and found

*Eric Mezy, Paris, France*

Eric could not rest. During the day and at night, when he was awake and while he slept, Eric was cursed by a restless spirit. It was driving him out of his mind with madness. No matter how hard he tried he could not stop thinking about the money. He even dreamt about it, three times now. Each time, he woke up in a wild state of panic – someone had found the money. Then he would laugh and say to himself, 'It's just a dream Eric, just a dream', and pat his chest in mock relief to make sure his heart was still beating. Was there no end to this torture?

At the age of twenty-seven Eric finally went ahead and did what he had been planning to do for years. He broke into the mission next door to the flat where he lived and stole what to him was a lot of money – 1,000 dollars. He was shocked to find American notes in the cash box on the desk in the back room which he could see from the window of his flat.

He had expected to find French currency, what

else? But he was sure he could change it, probably in Paris at the *bureau de change*. He could pretend he was a tourist, or something like that. Anyway, dollars or not, it was cash and cash was what he needed, so Eric stashed what he had taken in a hole in a tree in the garden of an empty house in the next street and then went home to think.

It was at this point that Eric started drinking heavily, probably to celebrate his ill-gotten gain, and everything went wrong. He told a friend what he had done, swearing her to secrecy, and within forty-eight hours was sitting in an interrogation cell at a police station confessing his crime to a detective. He was sent to court, where the judge had a reputation for handing out severe sentences, and ended up sharing a cell in a remand prison with an ex-wrestler while the detective searched for the missing cash box.

Eric told the police there were only fifty francs in the cash box and he spent them immediately on food and drink. He said he could not remember where he left the cash box, hoping that it would still be in the hole in the tree when he finally got out of jail. The police did not believe him and the mission insisted that 1,000 dollars was missing. It was a donation from a visiting pastor, who had come all the way from Kansas to see a sick friend.

So Eric sat in his cell listening to the wrestler snoring, worried sick that he could end up behind bars for months, maybe longer. Part of him wished he hadn't done it, but most of him kept thinking about the money and what he would spend it on

# LOST AND FOUND

when he got out. He was not sorry. He didn't care at all.

Two days later he was sitting in his cell and a preacher came by. He was French, from the south, and something about him impressed Eric.

'Do I know you?' Eric asked.

'No,' said the preacher. 'We have not met before but I must tell you that I have seen your face before, in a dream. That is why I am here. God has sent me to tell you to put right the wrong you have done. Eric, you must return the money you stole from the mission.'

Eric was speechless. He turned to look at the wrestler but he was sleeping. The preacher just stood there smiling. 'I, you, how, who,' the words came out jumbled and stuttering and Eric's heart was beating quickly and his mouth was dry and he just sat there trembling and scared.

'Do you want to go to the chapel?' asked the preacher.

Eric just nodded. The two men were allowed to go to the prison chapel where the preacher told Eric about the dream and about the love of Jesus and the forgiveness of sins.

'You mean to tell me that God showed you who I was and led you here to the prison?' Eric asked, still in a state of shock.

'Yes he did. The mission called to tell me about the robbery and asked me to pray for them. I did and now I'm here to ask you two things. Will you take the money back and do you want God?'

Eric's heart was suddenly moved in a new way and for the first time ever he felt ashamed. 'Yes I want God,' he said.

'What about the money?'

Eric looked at the preacher. He was not smiling any more. 'But I told the police I only took fifty francs, and anyway I may not be able to give it back. I've still got . . .'

The preacher put two fingers to Eric's lips. 'Hush, I do not want to know any more. If you trust God he will not let you down.'

So Eric committed his life to God there and then and asked Jesus to come in and be his Lord and Saviour. Twenty-four hours later he was released from prison.

Eric took the cash box and the 1,000 dollars back to the mission and confessed to the robbery. The manager of the mission thanked Eric for his honesty and rewarded him by giving him a job. Eric is still there to this day as a fund raiser.

# 4

# Man in black

*Anonymous*

Tom had ten seconds to live, maybe less. He felt the cold steel rim of the gun barrel press hard against the back of his head. The man in black was counting backwards; 'ten, nine, eight . . .' Tom was roped to a chair, blindfolded and gagged, and he clenched his teeth and tensed every muscle as the man in black continued 'seven, six, five, four'. Cold sweat ran down the back of Tom's neck and the man in black touched the clammy skin as he pushed the other man's head forward turning the gun slightly, pushing it behind Tom's right ear. 'Three, two', Tom let out a muffled scream, 'One; see you in hell, scum'. The man in black licked his top lip and pulled the trigger. Tom's head exploded.

The bed sheet was wet with sweat where Tom had tossed and turned and there was blood on the pillow. The nightmare had seemed so real that his most primal reflex action, a subliminal fight or flight mechanism, was activated by the gun shot. Tom, face down when the man in black had pulled the trigger, twisted violently as he lurched back into consciousness, smashing his cheek on the metal frame of the bed.

He sat up and wiped blood from his face, fingers trembling as he felt the raised edges of the small gash. He was still sweating, and stinging rivulets of perspiration seeped into his eyes and into the wound. Tom shivered as the last chilling dark waves of the nightmare slipped away and disappeared beneath the surface of reality. He closed his eyes. He wasn't scared now: just a bad dream, another bad dream, he thought.

It was the second night running that Tom had dreamt about the man in black. The first time he had leapt out of his bed and ended up sprawling across the floor of his prison cell face down on the cold floor, the end of a terrifying pursuit across a desolate dreamscape that appeared to stretch for an eternity in the horror of space and terror of time within Tom's troubled subconsciousness.

Fragments of the nightmare; diffused particles of memory had drifted in and out of his mind as he waited for the morning call to slop out. He was tired after losing a night's sleep but he knew he could not sleep even if he was left in his cell all day. He could not stop thinking about the man in black, his black hooded mask and black leather gloves pulled tight over murdering hands.

Tom shut his eyes tight to try and squeeze out the awful memory, but more terrible images flooded his troubled mind: bomb blasts and gun shots, blood and flesh and body parts of screaming women and children, men writhing in pain and the man in black watching with eyes dark and cold, uncaring, without mercy.

The sound of the key in the cell door brought Tom back to his senses but the look in the eye of the prison guard reminded him of the awful reality of his situation. 'If looks could kill . . .' he thought, 'but after what I have done I guess I don't blame him.'

Tom started the long walk down the corridor and stairs to the toilets where his day started with the pungent smell of the previous night's urine and excrement being washed down the sluices.

He had been inside for seven years and was used to the routine, but he hated being locked up, caged like some kind of animal. But he was an animal, at least that is how the judge had described him before giving him a life sentence following his conviction for terrorism.

The truth hurt and it would for a long time, for ever perhaps. The real torture though was in the nightmares because in reality Tom was the man in black, or had been. He had killed and tortured, executed, pressed the gun hard and brutally into the back of his victims' necks and pulled the trigger. He was a convicted terrorist, or to put it as the judge had, a cold-blooded murderer.

The words came back to haunt him frequently and now the dreams were haunting him too. He would surely go insane like some of the hardest men he knew inside, those who could not cope with being locked up or with the guilt which was the real killer.

Guilt like a cancer, eating away inside you, gnawing at your soul and tearing up the very fibre of your heart and mind. Guilt betrayed Tom just as it betrayed others, who ended up crying in dark cells trying to remember the reason why they had killed.

Tom became involved with terrorism shortly after the troubles began in Northern Ireland in the late 1960s. Three decades and gallons of innocent blood later he finally realised the truth, and it was not the same as the truth he believed when he first had to make a choice as to what was right and what was wrong.

He was a young man then and, with a passion burning in his heart, did not doubt that choosing to pledge his allegiance to a paramilitary organisation was the right thing to do. If only he had known then what he knew now; God did not support any of the factions fighting in the province but wanted peace instead, the same peace that Tom now had in his heart.

Tom had been raised as a Protestant. He felt he was British and joined the Loyalists who wanted to see Northern Ireland remain part of the United Kingdom, but by the time he was twenty-seven he found himself in the high-security Maze Prison.

It was following a meeting with a visiting missionary that Tom stopped talking about guns and bombs and revenge. 'Suddenly I realised that God was not on the side of the Loyalists,' he recalled.

'They say they are fighting for God and Ulster

while the Republicans say they are fighting for God and Ireland. But I realised that God was on no side and we were not on his. The missionary talked to me about Jesus and what he stood for. I spent a lot of time in my cell trying to understand why it had made me feel so strange inside.

'I could not stop thinking about God, so I started talking to the prison chaplain and other Christian inmates, some of whom were former terrorists who had found peace in God, and then I decided to go to the prison's Bible classes.

'I was so convicted and so confused. Everything I had ever believed did not mean that much to me any more. Something was happening to me, something amazing.'

But it was only after he had talked to a former member of the Irish Republican Army whose wife and young son had been murdered by Loyalist terrorists that Tom knew he had to give his life to Jesus. And when he did so, seven years into his sentence, his life changed dramatically.

'I could have tortured myself with my past for the rest of my life,' he later said to the missionary who, years earlier, had first told him about the love of God. 'The guilt and then the dreams, it was hell, absolute hell, but I've had to leave it all to God and I know he has forgiven me.'

There are still times when Tom thinks about what happened to his victims, those he killed and maimed. And the nightmares sometimes return to disturb his sleep. 'I sank to the depths of the darkest hell to do what I did to innocent people,' he admits, 'but God still loved me and gave his son Jesus to take away my sins. When I came to him I saw that love; it's the only reason why I can carry on.'

Tom was due for release from prison in 1996. He planned to travel to Africa to help missions share the gospel.

# 5

# Soul-hole

*Betty Wilson, Julia Tutwiler Prison for Women,
Alabama, USA*

There are days when Betty Wilson wishes she was on Death Row because then, when your appeals have been exhausted, there is an end to the awful torture of a limbo existence in which the inmate is forgotten by the legal system but not disposed of physically. People like Betty Wilson are in effect, buried alive.

Betty was sentenced to life without parole – America's alternative to the death penalty for murder – for hiring a killer to murder her millionaire husband in order to claim his insurance money. She says she is innocent and was hated locally for being a 'rich bitch' and a 'liberal'.

The hit-man, John Brown, confessed that her identical sister asked him to do the killing. He later retracted his statement, and the twin was acquitted and Betty went to jail.

An elegant woman in her early fifties with glossy brown hair, Betty says that at her trial her affair with a black American was used to prejudice the white jury against her.

Inside she was sexually assaulted by a group of black American inmates. 'It's a power thing,' she says. 'They will stand in the halls and masturbate – there's no shame, no pride, no dignity.

'They prostitute themselves in here, and it's nothing to do with love or even liking. Some do it for a cigarette, and for others it's to teach someone a lesson. I don't have any friends and at first I used to find prison existence unbearable.

'I thought about killing myself because when you are looking at twenty to twenty-five years without any chance of parole, hope just drains away, as though there is a hole in your soul. But one day I had a conversation with a Roman Catholic nun who said God had not forsaken me. Those few words changed my life, maybe even saved it.

'She was a spiritual advisor to the inmates on Death Row and those who were facing life without parole, but I had no faith in God at all and did not want anything to do with religion.

'But at my lowest point I needed someone to talk to and she was there to listen. She prayed with me and gave me a Bible. I read it from cover to cover in less than a month and finally I realised I had found the key to my own salvation.

'Spending the rest of your natural life in prison is worse than death itself, unless you have faith and hope in God. I have put all my trust in him. Sometimes you have to hit rock bottom and be

## SOUL-HOLE

stripped of everything right down to your naked soul before you realise that God is the most important thing. Without him we are nothing.'

# 6

# Shark-eyes

*Carlos Garcia, Miami State Penitentiary, Florida, USA*

The man bending over the wash basin, spitting blood and staring at his hard-faced reflection in the cracked mirror, was known by everyone in the prison as Shark-eyes.

His were cold, black and lifeless. Dolls' eyes. Eyes you would not wish to look into. Eyes that had men and women killed, brutally, sadistically, without remorse, sometimes for fun.

Shark-eyes had hate written all over his disfigured stony slab of a face and as he looked in the mirror he saw the devil looking back. But this time the reflection scared him and Shark-eyes had never been scared before in his life.

For the first time he was terrified of death. He saw evil and desperation and every bad thing that a man could possibly be and still live to taste the poison slowly killing him. Shark-eyes did not recognise himself.

He was no more, just a shell of a man whose body, mind, and soul had been stripped of any goodness and filled with deception, greed and lust, and so hideously distorted that even when he closed and squeezed his eyes tight and tried to remember who he was the face in the mirror still looked back and smiled when all he wanted to do was cry.

When he arrived at the prison to serve a life sentence for smuggling heroin after rebuilding his collapsed drugs empire Shark-eyes was feared by every man inside, even the guards.

His reputation had gone before him, and rumours and whispers of Mafia executions and other killings spread like a creeping fog along every corridor and into every cell where other murderers and thieves spoke in hushed voices about Shark-eyes and whether his victims numbered fifty, hundreds, or a thousand.

No one knew for sure because there was never enough evidence to convict Shark-eyes of murder. At first no one approached him, except for the guards, but even they were cautious and said or did no more than was required of them. They did not make eye contact with him, or stand too close to him. No one walked past him or asked him to move.

Shark-eyes was first to slop out in the morning and first to eat. He sat alone at mealtimes and no one sat next to him in the library or recreation room.

In the exercise yard one afternoon another prisoner who was a violent killer bumped into Shark-eyes. Some said it was an accident, others said it was an act of provocation, a challenge and a confrontation between two men who were feared the most.

One was daring the other, testing his strength,

## SHARK-EYES

throwing down the gauntlet. Shark-eyes stopped walking and stood still, head down, looking at the ground. The killer moved in close to Shark-eyes. He was taller and more heavily built and there was no fear in his eyes as he loomed aggressively over the other man, fists clenched and bone hard with white scars like seams of granite in stone.

Shark-eyes was still like a statue, cold and without emotion, and when he moved to turn and raise his head to look at the killer it was as though time had slowed right down and the space around the two men was heavy and spellbound with Shark-eyes controlling every movement and thought, sapping the strength and soul of the killer whose gaze now wavered and flickered with dread.

Shark-eyes raised his hand and made the shape of a gun with two fingers bent in and two fingers pointed as the barrel and thumb cocked like a hammer-trigger. He pushed the finger-gun hard into the killer's temple, moved his thumb down and made a clicking noise. 'Next time it will be loaded,' he whispered.

It happened so quickly and the guards were slow to react. By the time they reached the two men the killer was on his knees crying and Shark-eyes was walking again. The killer cried for two weeks and was eventually transferred to the psychiatric wing of the prison and the rumours and whispers spread like a creeping fog again, but this time no one doubted.

No one saw Shark-eyes crying or his tears falling and splashing on the metal sink as he looked in the mirror and wished the devil looking back would place a gun against his head and snap the hammer-trigger down.

Shark-eyes had spent twenty years getting rich and powerful, by fraud and deception and killing, only to find that all that was of no value when his world fell apart, and he was so terrified of death that he was desperate to do anything to find an answer before he was consumed and lost completely in the darkness in the eyes of the face in the mirror.

Shortly after the confrontation with the killer in the exercise yard Shark-eyes was attracted by the sound of singing in the chapel down the corridor and asked a guard if he could join one of the Christian classes.

He had such a cynical and malevolent nature that the prison warder at first refused, but the Roman Catholic priest in charge of the chapel gave him a Bible and later invited him to the group.

Then one night Shark-eyes dreamed he had died and gone to hell and it was so real and frightened him so much that afterwards he was determined to change. Two days later he woke up in the middle of the night in tears and deeply disturbed. He could not stop shaking and his hands trembled as he picked up the Bible and read right through the Book of Psalms where it had fallen open in his hands, and one particular psalm struck him with such force it seemed to jump out of the pages at him:

[1]Give ear to my words, O LORD, consider my meditation. [2]Hearken unto the voice of my cry, my

## SHARK-EYES

King, and my God: for unto thee will I pray. ³My voice shalt thou hear in the morning, O Lord; in the morning will I direct my prayer unto thee, and will look up. ⁴For thou art not a God that hath pleasure in wickedness: neither shall evil dwell with thee. ⁵The foolish shall not stand in thy sight: thou hatest all workers of iniquity. ⁶That shalt destroy them that speak leasing: the Lord will abhor the bloody and deceitful man. ⁷But as for me, I will come into thy house in the multitude of thy mercy: and in thy fear I will worship toward thy holy temple. ⁸Lead me, O Lord, in thy righteousness because of mine enemies; make thy way straight before my face. ⁹For there is no faithfulness in their mouth; their inward part is very wickedness; their throat is an open sepulchre; they flatter with their tongue. ¹⁰Destroy thou them, O God; let them fall by their own counsels; cast them out in the multitude of their transgressions; for they have rebelled against thee. ¹¹But let all those that put their trust in thee rejoice: let them ever shout for joy, because thou defendest them: let them also that love thy name be joyful in thee. ¹²For thou, Lord, wilt bless the righteous; with favour wilt thou compass him with a shield (Ps. 5 KJV).

Shark-eyes wiped away his tears. Here was the answer in black and white – righteousness was the key to his salvation; he realised that God was the only one who could give it to him and he invited the Lord into his life.

## GOSPEL BEHIND BARS

He was filled with happiness and had such inner peace that he actually enjoyed being in prison for the rest of his sentence. He became a trustee of the chapel, studied the Bible daily and prayed morning and night. After a time he earned early parole, married a widow in the church he joined and eventually they established a mission for ex-convicts.

Shark-eyes kept clear of trouble and never returned to his life of crime; those he once may have had killed came to him for counselling and would look into his kind eyes and see love and compassion and the grace of God reflecting back.

# 7

# The Pig

*Giovanni Brusea, Florence Prison, Italy*

This is Giovanni's story. It is sad and terrible in places and no matter how brave and honest Giovanni becomes as the story unfolds you can never love him with the love he received one night as he waited to die.

Giovanni was waiting to die because he had taken the biggest risk and done the bravest, most honest thing of his bad life; giving evidence to the police which would convict a Mafia leader who had been involved in more than 3,000 murders.

Murder 3,001 would be his own, Giovanni was sure of it. He had turned supergrass and even though he was now locked in a high-security cell he feared for his life.

Franko 'The Dog' Berro, Giovanni's former Mafia boss and mentor, could get to anyone, no matter how well they were guarded. Giovanni had seen him do it and had done it himself; killing men in prison and in police custody or in hiding was no problem. 'The Dog' knew a lot of people, he had influence, a lot of influence, even with the police. He was the boss of all bosses and as sure as night followed day he would get to Giovanni.

Every footstep, every shadow, every other noise of the night made Giovanni's heart beat faster. At sixty he was sure the pressure would kill him before 'The Dog' did and the only thing he had to ease his fear was a small red Bible and the cross of gold around his neck.

Like many Italians Giovanni was raised as a Catholic but he stopped believing in God the day he met 'The Dog'. Then he became God and Giovanni became his brutal lieutenant, nicknamed 'The Pig', and he revelled in his role in the reign of terror they held over their own small area of Italy.

'The Dog' was the brains behind all the killings but Giovanni 'The Pig' was the ruthless one. He and 'The Dog's' other Mafia 'animals' killed without remorse; tortured for sadistic pleasure. Once a family of four were murdered as they slept and 'The Pig' laughed when he saw television pictures of the carnage.

'He was a sick son of a bitch,' one of 'The Dog's' other men said after hearing 'The Pig' had found God before turning supergrass. 'No one liked him, even Franko Berro thought he was an animal, but he was good at his job and you could trust him, or so they thought.'

Giovanni was loyal to Franko for more than thirty years and it is claimed that Giovanni even had his own brother killed because 'The Dog' said he was an

# THE PIG

informer. That was the one thing Giovanni hated: a grass. Anyone who informed on the Mafia deserved to die, slowly and painfully. They found what they could only guess was Giovanni's brother's torso in a deep freeze. They never found the rest of him.

But after 'The Dog' had ordered the execution of a rival Mafia member something happened to Giovanni that changed everything. Giovanni had been arrested and held in police custody on a charge of suspicion of murder, which everyone knew would not hold up in court. He had been paying bribes for 'The Dog' to senior officials for years anyway so charges were inevitably always dropped.

So 'The Pig', smoking a Nazionale cigarette, kindly donated by a police officer, was sitting in a cell waiting to go home when a young Catholic priest by the name of Salvatore came to the bars of the cell door and started talking.

He introduced himself and said he had been sent by someone more powerful than 'The Dog' to warn Giovanni to stop what he was doing and 'become an honest God-fearing man'.

'Who sent you? Who is more powerful than 'The Dog?' Giovanni asked.

'God,' Salvatore replied.

'Go away before I have you killed,' 'The Pig' said. 'Don't you know who I am?'

The priest said he did but would not leave until he had told Giovanni a remarkable story about a dream and a burning cross of gold. In the dream Giovanni had been shot and was dying. In his hand was the cross of gold that he always wore around his neck. The chain had snapped and he held the cross tightly, praying for mercy and life and asking God to forgive him for all the terrible things he had done.

'So?' 'The Pig' said. 'So what, I'm going to Hell, big deal.'

'Maybe,' said Salvatore, 'but I did not know who you were. You were in my dream but I did not recognise your face until earlier today when you were outside my church and the police were pushing you into a car. I remembered, you were the dying man in my dream and after they had taken you away I found this on the pavement.'

The priest reached into his pocket and pulled out Giovanni's chain and cross.

'What!' exclaimed 'The Pig', reaching for his neck and feeling for the chain and cross he believed he was still wearing. It was not there.

'You must have dropped it,' Salvatore said. 'Here take it; it is obviously important to you.'

The priest handed Giovanni the necklace through the bars and, without saying another word, disappeared.

A few minutes later a police officer came to 'The Pig's' cell. 'Have another smoke,' he said, offering a cigarette through the bars.

'No. Just get me out of here,' The Pig whispered, still looking at the chain and cross in the palm of his trembling hand.

'Sorry, I can't do that,' the police officer replied.

## THE PIG

'You have to stay here overnight but you will be out in the morning.'

'The Pig' could not believe what was happening to him, but later that night something else happened, a miracle which touched the very fibre of Giovanni's soul and brought him to his knees crying and begging for redemption from his awful life of crime.

It was after midnight and he could not sleep. He kept thinking about the priest and 'The Dog' and why the police had detained him for longer than usual, when suddenly he was gripped by intense pain in his chest and shoulder. He was having a heart attack.

'The Pig' gasped and tried to sit up but could not and the pain was so bad it felt as if his heart was being crushed in a vice which was getting tighter and tighter until he could hardly breathe. Then he passed out.

When he came round the pain had gone but he was aware of a new sensation. He was tingling all over as if he was having some kind of mild electric shock, and then he saw the light, a faint golden glow at first and then brighter until it was like a small fire burning fiercely in the corner of his cell.

Giovanni watched the dancing golden flames grow higher until they were as high as the cell wall. He was frightened but could not move or speak and just lay motionless on the bed watching the strange apparition increase in size until it consumed the whole of the cell, until he feared he too would be consumed.

Then Giovanni heard the voice. A still, small voice,

no more than a whisper but unmistakably clear. It came out of the light and Giovanni trembled as he shielded his eyes from the intensity of brightness; it was brighter than the sun and now he could feel heat on his face, real heat, and he buried his face in his pillow and listened.

'Pin back your ears Giovanni and heed the Word of the Lord. Turn from your evil ways and seek the Lord while he may still be found.'

Giovanni got off the bed and fell to his knees. His eyes were closed but he could still feel the warmth of the light and again the voice spoke.

'God loves you Giovanni. He longs to be in fellowship with you. Turn your eyes from darkness unto his light. Know the truth and it shall set you free.'

And then it was gone. The light disappeared, the cell was dark again and Giovanni started to cry. He cried himself to sleep and when he awoke he was lying on the floor and he could hear another voice, but this time it was the police guard telling him to get up.

'It's time to go,' he said. 'They want you in court in an hour.'

Giovanni got to his feet. 'Give me ten minutes,' he replied, 'and get me a priest, the one who came to see me yesterday. It's very important; I have to see him.'

'You have a confession to make?' The guard laughed. 'Or is he on the payroll too? I guess even God can be bribed, eh?'

# THE PIG

Giovanni ignored the joke. 'Just get the priest, now,' he snapped and the guard quickly remembered who was talking and scuttled off down the corridor.

Salvatore the priest arrived an hour later. Giovanni was pacing up and down in his cell. 'Thank God,' he said when he saw the familiar face.

'They say I have only five minutes before you go to court. Can I help you in any way?'

'I hope so,' Giovanni said and started to tell Salvatore about what happened to him during the night.

'And you believe it was a warning from God?' the priest asked.

'Yes, yes I do. The voice was so clear and I could feel the presence of someone in the room. I think God sent an angel to my cell.'

'You look different,' Salvatore said, reaching his hand through the bars. 'Come here Giovanni, I wish to pray with you.'

Giovanni moved closer and the priest placed his hand on the other man's head and together they prayed.

It was the first time Giovanni had prayed since he was a young man and he felt as though a huge weight was being lifted off him as he asked God to forgive him.

'It's the weight of sin being removed from your soul,' the priest said afterwards. 'You are a changed man now Giovanni and you must live a new life. God has saved you, now you must honour him with your life.'

'I will,' he replied, and with that Salvatore left and Giovanni sat on the edge of his bed and whispered, 'God I believe what has happened to me is a miracle and because I want to honour you I will turn from my life of crime, starting now.'

Later that morning Giovanni went to court and confessed to his involvement in the murder of the rival Mafia member and a few hours later gave evidence which would convict 'The Dog' and many of the men who worked for him.

The police were shocked. They could not believe 'The Pig' had turned. 'Why are you doing this?' they asked.

'Because God wants me to,' came the reply.

Giovanni was sentenced to imprisonment with the rest of the Mafia. He survived two attempts on his life while in jail. He was eventually transferred under a false name to another prison where he studied theology and later became an assistant to the chaplain.

# 8

# Reality

*Nancy Beckenridge, Julia Tutwiler Prison for Women, Alabama, USA*

Before Nancy became a Christian she longed for one of those virtual reality machines. You know the sort I mean – a futuristic helmet like Arnold Schwarzenegger used to holiday on Mars in the film *Total Recall* – only Nancy's machine would have taken her horse riding high up into the Rockies above soaring eagles and the Continental Divide.

Better still she would tear down the bars of the steel cage around her and walk right out of this hellhole, right out past Death Row, the killing cell and the electric chair, past the white morning glory blooming sweetly between the steps leading into the light, and past the high fences to run with the wild horses and never stop.

Nancy used to train horses before she was jailed for killing her lover's wife. Now, in her mid-forties, she claims that she is innocent but her appeals process has run out and she can expect to spend the rest of her life in her ten foot by eight foot cell.

'There were times when I longed to be on Death Row,' she says. 'It's quiet there and you know what is going to happen. Accepting the reality of my situation is difficult but not as difficult as accepting its permanence. I know what it is to feel free. I can still feel the wind rushing by as I ride the high country, twelve thousand feet up, so high you can almost touch heaven. God, I long to feel free again.'

Many believe life without parole is worse than death itself. It means a limbo existence. They call people on Death Row 'living dead' but the same can be said of those buried alive in a place where there is no hope. The dehumanising process of waiting for state-inflicted death is too awful to imagine, but it is not heard to understand why some are terrified that their death sentence will be changed to life without parole.

Nancy's husband, whom she met while facing trial, has not been able to accept life without parole. He was arrested while planning to get her out by blowing up the prison. He could not deal with Nancy's being locked up for the rest of her life, and he fired shots when he was arrested and was shot in the back. So now he's paralysed and was sentenced to nineteen years in a federal jail.

The couple have not been allowed any contact with each other since 1994, and Nancy is allowed to see her eleven-year-old daughter only once a year.

'I started to lose my mind,' she recalls. 'I really thought I was going insane. It was breakfast in my cell at 4 a.m., lunch at 9.30 and dinner at 2.30. The

# REALITY

rest of the time I spent making dolls and crochet animals and was thinking seriously about loading up with Thorazine.

'It's a drug that turns you into a zombie. It's available to everyone doing life, but after a while you're hooked and you might as well be dead, which can be quite appealing to someone condemned to solitary confinement and facing life with no chance of parole.

'But something changed my mind. I was reading books on philosophy and other spiritual material when I was given a book called *The Cross and the Switchblade*, the story of the dramatic conversion of New York gang leader Nicky Cruz. I never thought about God or religion before but suddenly I was thinking about Jesus all the time, who he was and what did he mean to me.

'A Sister who was a spiritual adviser at the prison later talked to me about Jesus and through her influence I asked for a Bible, which I read cover to cover in a few weeks. I could not put it down and when I started reading about the crucifixion I knew I had to give my life to Jesus. When I did I knew I had been forgiven.

'I really could have tortured myself with my past and gone completely crazy worrying about the future but I have had to leave it all to God and I know he will help me. I pray every day and study the Bible and have hope now, even though my circumstances have not changed. When I close my eyes and see his face my spirit soars higher than the Rockies. That is my freedom now.'

# 9

# Dead man walking

*Anonymous*

This is a story about what happened to Paul Jonssen during the last few hours of his life. It is a sad story because there is no happy ending. No winners, only losers.

One man kills and then he is killed. Someone loses a mother and a mother loses a son. There is good and there is evil and sometimes the latter destroys the other and then is also destroyed to complete a circle that starts with life and ends with death.

Paul Jonssen was born and lived and killed and was killed. Period. Except that just before he died Paul Jonssen witnessed a miracle and the change that came over him during the last few hours of his life was remarkable.

It is said, and with some truth, that a man facing death thinks more about his past than his future, especially if he believed in life after death. Maybe it should be the other way round, and that a man who believes death is nothing more than an exit to eternity would be preoccupied with destination.

But it is not like that, or so I am told by those who have heard and remember the final words of the men whose last walk on earth has been to the electric chair or gas chamber or gallows. Dead men walking almost always look back.

Perhaps it is the final realisation that you can't turn back time. It just doesn't happen. We all make mistakes. Some live with them and others die because of them. But there is always some element of regret and some thread of truth that leads us back to the past where we wish upon wish for the power to reanimate the shadows of experience.

Paul Jonssen wished this over and over again but one day he stopped and said: 'I am not God and I don't believe in God so I can only remember my past and see where it leads to a dead-end with no way forward or back.'

Paul Jonssen spent eleven years in an eight foot by six foot cell on Death Row for stabbing a woman to death. At the time he was thirty, a good-looking, intelligent white American with a future. No one really knows why he did it. Maybe he was a victim of circumstance, maybe not. But he did commit murder and was convicted and then condemned to death by lethal injection.

In the beginning when he first arrived on Death Row Paul Jonssen was an atheist. The last time he had read from the Bible or attended church was years ago when he was a small boy. Even then he did not believe in God or heaven, and hell was only one of those places he hated to be such as in school or the dentist's chair or locked in his bedroom on those long days when he was grounded and he could hear his friends playing ball outside.

That was the worst thing. Being locked up, like an animal in a cage. No way out, completely trapped. There was no tomorrow when everything would be okay and he wasn't grounded any longer, no second, third or fourth chance. No sorry I won't do it again, no happy ever after.

It would end with a lethal injection of poison and the end would come, but not when he expected it. And the waiting made him very afraid, more afraid than the execution itself because he believed it would be painless and quick, 'like snuffing out a candle flame with wet fingertips,' he said.

Paul Jonssen had already had three execution dates before the end of his life: the last time he had been just seven hours away from death before he received a stay of execution. 'They were the darkest hours,' he wrote in a final letter to a friend.

'I wanted to die, and each time I received a stay of execution. I felt I could not possibly survive until the next time. But today I found out the reason why I am being kept alive. It is to make sure I know where I am going afterwards and that place is heaven.'

It was the first time in his life that Paul Jonssen had believed in life after death, but what happened to him in his cell three days before his final execution date was so amazing, so incredible, that even the most unshakeable atheist would have been moved to believe. Paul Jonssen was visited by an angel and it was so real that a prison guard saw it too.

It was late and the night lights in the cells on Death Row flickered and cast shadows through the bars and across the metal corridor where the prison guard stood checking his watch waiting for his shift to end. Then it happened. A bright light from one of the cells startled him. For a second he thought fire, but in the few moments it took him to reach the front of Paul Jonssen's cell he knew he was dealing with something much more terrifying.

Right there inside the cell a tall winged being, glowing like a furnace, stood over Paul Jonssen's bed and then suddenly it was gone. The guard blinked and grabbed the steel bars of the cell door to steady himself. He closed his eyes and looked again. Nothing. 'Are you all right?' he asked, his voice a whisper. 'Yes' came the reply. 'Are you?'

The guard did not report the incident. He was scared of being ridiculed by his fellow officers. Instead the next night, the eve of Paul's Jonssen's execution, he went back to the cell and asked if what he had seen the night before had been real. 'Yes. You saw an angel,' Paul Jonssen said. 'It was real. It said "Fear not for God is with you." '

'It spoke,' said the guard. 'Well, sweet Jesus I don't believe it.'

The next day Paul Jonssen was prepared for the execution. His limbs were strapped down and he had the injection tube in his arm. He had a clean white uniform. The executioners were hidden behind a two-way mirror. There was a clock on the wall and a chaplain stood next to him. Then he made his statement.

'Last night I accepted Jesus Christ as my saviour. This will not bring your loved one back but God has forgiven me and now I am ready to be with him.' Paul Jonssen made eye contact with the chaplain, then he looked towards the ceiling, took a deep breath and said: 'Do it.' His body rose and he gasped as his lungs relaxed to expel his last breath.

# 10

# Feel the sun

❧

*Charles Gains, Monterey, California, USA*

Charles was a half Blackfoot Indian and his father Jackson was full blooded. In 1960 Charles killed his father and then tried to kill himself. It happened quickly and without warning and shocked everyone who knew the two men.

No one knows for sure exactly what took place on that cold winter night inside the wooden house on the banks of the Great Falls river where Jackson and his blind twenty-year-old son Charles lived.

Charles, almost seven feet tall, was drunk on whiskey and stabbed Jackson through the heart with a ten-inch hunting knife before staggering outside and throwing himself in the river. He almost drowned and, when a farmer found his body washed up on a sandbank a mile downstream, he thought he was looking at a corpse.

Where all this took place was in the remote part of Montana near the Canada border. Wheat-farming country. Jackson, whose first wife was Irish and died in a fire when Charles was ten, worked for a wheat

# GOSPEL BEHIND BARS

farmer and later had an affair with the farmer's wife.

Charles, who was blind from birth and blamed his father for the death of his mother, went crazy when he smelled perfume on Jackson and plunged the blade through his chest, spearing him to the kitchen table.

Jackson had stayed the day in the motel in town and was late home and the chicken stew which blind Charles had tried to heat on the stove was burnt as well as his hands. When his father arrived he grabbed the hot pan in a violent rage and threw it across the room.

What happened next ended with Jackson dead and Charles convicted of murder and sentenced to life in jail. The fact that Charles was blind and suffering a severe beating from his father when he used all his force to drive the blade through flesh and bone and wood persuaded the judge to rule out the death sentence but Charles showed no remorse at the trial and the court recommended life without parole.

He confessed everything, even how he kicked and jumped up and down on his father's blood-soaked body 'just to make sure he was properly dead', and how he had hidden the knife inside his boot and wrestled Jackson to the ground, feeling for the breastbone so he knew exactly where to stab.

They asked Charles 'why' many times and he gave the same answer over and over again. 'It wasn't the drink,' he'd say with a shake of the head, 'I could not forgive him for killing Mother Bear.'

Mother Bear was the name Charles called his

# FEEL THE SUN

mother, whose real name was Marie and who drowned in the Great Falls river. She had a fight with Jackson, fell into the river and banged her head on a rock; the current took her under and half a mile downstream.

They had been fishing and Jackson had got drunk on potato wine. Charles sat on a log away from the water's edge and heard his father shouting and swearing and then afterwards when it was quiet and he could no longer hear his mother's voice he felt Jackson's hand on his head. He smelled the sweet alcohol breath warm on his skin and a whispered warning not to tell anyone what he had heard.

Charles kept asking, 'What have you done to Mother Bear, where is she?'

Now he sat in his prison cell with the cold grey walls closing in and a black fly buzzing around a grimy light bulb and tried to remember how it felt to be safe in the warm embrace of his mother's arms. He listened to the chink chink of the fly hitting the light bulb and looked up to where he thought it was.

He had been taught by Mother Bear to imagine light. 'Feel the sun on your face and open your eyes to let it inside,' she told him. 'Now close your eyes and let the sun fill your body and it will guide you wherever you are.'

Charles stood and reached up, groping wildly for the light bulb. When he found it he squeezed and crushed the glass, extinguishing the light in his big hand, which was already burnt and now bled until the blood ran down his arm and under the cuff of his shirt.

That night Charles cried and told the guard he wanted to die. For a gold ring the guard promised to deliver a razor blade which he joked would not be as big as the hunting blade which killed Jackson but just as deadly.

Charles would cut his throat as soon as he had the blade. He did not want to live any more and was not afraid of dying. He had made up his mind, there would be no stopping him as long as the guard kept his promise.

But that night Charles dreamt he had died and gone to hell, only hell was under the surface of the Great Falls river where his mother floated, all white and skin and bone with wide eyes and open mouth and a gash in her head the size of a small rock.

Charles opened his mouth to scream and began to choke while his mother smiled, but woke before the water filled his lungs and sat bolt upright in bed sweating. He was shaking and put his head between his knees and rocked back and forth. It was then that it happened: a miracle. His blind eyes began to tingle and then burn and suddenly he could see. Darkness, not as black as the blindness, with shapes and shadows and a soft glowing light that made Charles snap his eyes tightly shut and grip the sides of the bed until the whites of his knuckles could be seen.

He shook his head from side to side and moaned out loud. 'Oh Mother Bear, Mother Bear, I'm so afraid, so afraid.' Charles clenched his teeth and opened one eye. The light was brighter and he quickly closed his eye and put his hands up to his face spreading his fingers over his eyes so he could peep at the thing which was making him so afraid. 'Oh, dear God, sweet Jesus, what can it be?' he whispered, slowly opening his eyes wide behind the protection of his hands.

'Oh Lord I can see,' he cried, and jumped to his feet and then fell to his knees as the light changed to fire and the fire to the outline of a man and then an angel with golden wings and burning eyes and hands that reached out and touched Charles's face.

Charles was silent and after a few moments his heart stopped racing and his body did not shake and there was only a slight tremble in his voice when he asked: 'Who are you? What do you want with me?'

The angel moved its hands from Charles's face to his shoulders and gently lifted him until he was standing. 'Don't be afraid,' the angel said, 'I have not come to harm you. I am here to tell you to worship the Lord God with all your heart and he will forgive you and keep a place for you in heaven.'

Charles felt tears forming and blinked and suddenly he was blind again. He closed his eyes and opened them but still there was nothing. He was blind again and he started to cry and fell on to the bed and cried himself to sleep.

He awoke to the sound of the guard hitting the bars of the cell with his stick. Charles got out of bed and stood facing the wrong way. 'I'm over here,' said the guard.

'I know,' Charles answered.

'Well turn around. I've got something for you.'

Charles turned to face the guard.

'Jesus,' the guard said. 'What happened to your eyes?'

Charles felt his eyes. 'Nothing happened,' he said.

'Something did,' the guard replied. 'They're all white and wide open like you can see or something crazy like that. What is it, an infection or something?'

'I told you there ain't nothing wrong and I don't want that blade any more.'

'I don't know what you're talking 'bout,' the guard snapped. 'You ain't getting no blade off me. Got something else though.'

Charles heard something drop to the floor and waited for the guard's footsteps to die away. He dropped to his knees and felt in front of him until he found what the guard had dropped through the bars. It was a book, a heavy book with a cover that felt like leather and pages so thick Charles thought they must be stuck together until he felt the tiny raised dots and realised he was feeling Braille. A Braille Bible.

He had learnt to read Braille when he was a child. He could not read it well but well enough to know that the book he was reading was a New Testament. In six months he had read it from cover to cover and was so convicted by the gospel message that he gave his life to Jesus.

Months later Charles died in his sleep. The coroner could not find anything wrong with him and settled for natural causes. Question mark: heart attack.

## FEEL THE SUN

But before he died Charles had told a visiting preacher that he was going to heaven, soon, and for the first time told the story of how he once saw an angel.

'I know,' said the preacher. 'I saw him too. He told me to send you a Bible.'

# 11

# Blood-release

*Sean Boyle, Maze Prison, Belfast, Northern Ireland*

At first Sean hated his younger brother Peter visiting him in prison. It was bad enough sitting out a two-year sentence, without being forced to listen to Christian talk about Jesus and love and forgiveness.

Peter's faith was contrary to everything Sean believed in and it made him angry. Before he was sent to prison Sean used to beat Peter because of his belief in God; now he could only sit and listen and afterwards smash his fist against the cell door in sheer frustration.

Sean did not want to hear about Jesus. He did not believe in him and even if he did he could never follow someone who preached peace and hated violence. 'At least I care enough to fight for what I believe in,' he thought. 'Christians have no courage, they are scared to stand up and fight and Jesus died because he let the Roman authorities walk all over him.'

But no one walked over Sean. He was tough and although he was prepared to die for the cause he would never surrender. 'The bastards will have to kill me to stop me fighting for what I believe is right,' he told Peter when he joined the IRA in his early twenties, so strong was his commitment to the Republican campaign.

As a member of the paramilitary Sean believed he was serving his country and God, if the Irish, like Peter, protested about people getting hurt or killed in the process, it was because they did not understand he was doing it for them.

Even when he was sent to prison for armed robbery which he did to help finance the IRA he did not doubt that the violent crimes were justified. Sean was a freedom fighter not a terrorist. 'I'm a hero,' he once claimed. 'They should give me a medal not a prison sentence.'

But although Sean tried to justify his terrorist activities, one thing kept coming back to haunt him while he served his prison sentence. 'When I was arrested the policeman said there would be a lot of people very happy,' he recalled, 'but I could not believe that because I was involved in the freedom process. The struggle was about important social issues as well as changing the colour of the flag.'

People had seen the side of Sean that was violent and aggressive, though, and their perception of a caring freedom fighter was different from that of the people living in the area.

'I believed there was nothing wrong in robbing a bank,' he added. 'It was just taking from the rich to give to the poor, and if people got hurt in the process

## BLOOD-RELEASE

of fighting for freedom, it was unfortunate but unavoidable. They were just casualties of war.

'But after listening to Peter I began to weigh up what Jesus said about stealing, violence and murder being wrong and for the first time in my life I found I could not defend my actions any more. I suddenly realised I had a caring heart but I had used it for evil.'

So Sean got on his knees and asked God to forgive him for all the bad things he had done and with tears running down his face gave his life to Jesus. After his release from prison he studied the Bible and became the leader of a Christian mission, preaching the gospel in Ireland and Europe and was never again involved with the IRA.

# 12

# Paper and fire

*Anonymous*

Brian Smith was converted to Christianity after physically feeling the agony of Christ on the cross as he looked at a picture of the crucifixion. It happened late one night several years ago when Smith was serving the seventh year of a life sentence for murder.

He killed a man in cold blood and could have ended up dying in jail. It was possible because the judge recommended a life sentence without parole and Smith was almost fifty when he committed his awful crime. He used to be scared of ending his own life behind bars, but after what happened to him during the weeks leading to Christmas in 1992 death no longer holds any fear for him.

Smith, who was sentenced in 1985, showed no remorse during his trial. It was one of the main reasons why many people at the time felt Smith deserved to die in prison. 'You should rot in hell for what you've done,' a friend of the murder victim screamed before spitting at Smith as they led him away from the courtroom.

## GOSPEL BEHIND BARS

He just smiled because he did not care. That was the way Smith was – evil – until the night of the miracle. The night when Smith experienced stigmata, marks like those on Christ's body after the crucifixion.

Before it happened Smith did not believe in God. He blasphemed more than most and had a nasty dislike for anyone connected with the Church, probably because his stepfather used to beat him. He was a lay preacher and believed in God and the horse-whip even though it took the flesh off young Brian Smith's back every other week, often before the wounds had healed. Smith shared his stepfather's violent temper and sadistic nature but none of his religious beliefs.

One week before Smith saw wounds on his wrists and feet he received two letters. One he opened immediately, the other he left unopened on the table in the corner of his prison cell. The second letter had a London postmark and Smith thought it was from his younger brother whom he hated. He was wrong, but he did not find out until the night of his dramatic conversion.

Inside the first letter was a small picture of the crucifixion. It looked as though it had been torn from a Bible and had a note attached to it. 'You don't know me but I'm praying for your salvation,' it said. 'Some kind of religious freak,' Smith thought and set fire to it with his cigarette and watched the tissue-thin paper turn to ash.

Six days later Smith opened the second letter and

was deeply shocked at what he found. It was another picture of the crucifixion, a vivid colour sketch on a neatly-folded piece of drawing paper. On the back someone had written, 'Christ died for your sins.'

Smith looked at the picture and imagined it must have been sent by the same person who sent the first letter and he screwed the paper up and crushed it in his clenched fist. 'Jesus,' he hissed, 'I'd like to get my hands on them.'

Suddenly his hands started to shake and then his arms and legs until he was shaking all over like someone shivering from severe cold. He could not stop and thought he was living some kind of heart attack so he quickly sat down on the edge of the bed and tried to control the shivering, but before he had time to think about what was happening it stopped as suddenly as it had begun.

Then the pain started. A burning sensation at first in his wrists and feet and then a deep aching and throbbing as though he had hurt himself in some way and was waiting for the swelling and bruising to appear.

But something else appeared instead, small wounds the size of penny coins, one on each wrist, and when he removed his shoes and socks to find out why his feet were hurting he discovered two more identical wounds. There was no blood, only dark angry puncture marks as though something had pierced his wrists and feet.

'Oh Jesus,' he whispered as he began to realise what was happening to him. 'Oh Jesus, Jesus Christ,' and he reached down to pick up the crumpled picture. 'This can't be happening, it can't be real.' But the wounds were still there and as he straightened out the paper they started to bleed. He fell to his knees and began to cry.

Through his tears Smith looked at the nails in Christ's hands and feet and could almost sense the agony. He looked at his own wounds and, convinced of God's presence, confessed to a lifetime of evil and asked for forgiveness for the first time in his life.

'It felt as if my sins were being lifted out of my body,' he recalled years later. 'It left me with a feeling of peace and I cried for joy for several hours afterwards. My own wounds disappeared. I did not even notice them go, but they were real, I know they were.'

From that night on Brian Smith wanted to do God's work and says he has not had a violent or malicious thought since. He spent the next few years studying the Bible and teaching fellow inmates about Christianity.

# 13

# Something to remind you

*Lucia Gordon, Julia Tutwiler Prison for Women,
Alabama, USA*

Lucia Gordon had tears in her eyes as she looked at the torn photograph. She was sitting on the edge of the bed in a motel room holding the faded picture gently in her trembling hands.

The tear cut across Nick Cohen's face, and she smoothed the paper flat trying to hide the imperfection. 'You're a handsome devil, Nick Cohen,' she sighed, tracing an outline with her index finger over the dark tousled hair, the high cheekbones, strong jawline and boyish smile.

She stopped to gaze into the eyes of the face in the photograph. 'Deep blue and wanting you'. The words came back to haunt her and she looked over her shoulder to where Nick Cohen's lifeless body lay slumped in an easy-back chair, blood seeping from a wound in his side where she had plunged a knife.

She looked away and closed her eyes and started to cry. A deep, painful sobbing that rent the very fibre of her soul. Her fingertips, red and raw where the nails had been bitten and torn away from the pink tender skin, dug into the faded picture, squeezing hard until it tore in half.

The deep blue of Nick Cohen's laughing eyes shone like heavenly planets in the swirling, dark mist of memory in Lucia's troubled mind. She squeezed her eyes shut tighter, closing out light, and took another drink of vodka to wash down the last of the sleeping tablets. The deep blue of Cohen's eyes started to fade, then suddenly without warning turned black.

They brought Lucia Gordon to the prison in leg-shackles and a belly chair. She was strip-searched and had to squat naked while guards probed her anus for drugs. She felt violated and threw up as they led her out of the white room and on to Death Row, the faces at the bars of the steel cages watching, some smiling at the dead woman walking.

Later, through the bars of her ten foot by eight foot cell Lucia's brown eyes stared out, expressionless, with pupils narrowed, at the guard standing outside. The shouting and screaming on the wings was loud but she could hear only the menacing whisper of the woman staring down at her.

'I'm going to tell you something bitch,' she said. 'I'm going tell you how you're gonna die. For stabbing that boy you're gonna feel the electric embrace of the Yellow Mamma. She's waiting for you bitch, waiting to fry your hide like a barbecued chicken. You get what I'm saying.'

Lucia did, but she did not respond. She turned around and reached behind her for the small plastic

## SOMETHING TO REMIND YOU

box containing her lipstick, mascara, and comb. She knew she was going to die for killing her boyfriend but she did not care as long as they did not take away her femininity. Her hand trembled as she combed her hair and smiled at the guard. 'You don't frighten me,' she thought and watched her walk away.

Convicted of stabbing to death Nick Cohen, her live-in boyfriend of six years, Lucia became one of four female living dead in a prison for women, outside a small town in the American mid-west. At the age of thirty-seven she believed she would be dead before her fiftieth birthday.

The woman in the next-door cell had been waiting to die for thirteen years after shooting her husband and Lucia knew she could be forced to wait as long, if not longer. She had already been told she would never again see her nine-year-old son and that her last walk would be to the chair.

Lucia's family had already disowned her, and her son was taken to live with his grandmother, who went to the trouble of writing one letter describing the 'justice of revenge'.

Lucia, dressed in her white prison-issue overall, laughed as she read. She was already loaded with the drug Thorazine and struggled to concentrate. 'Electrocution is the worst kind of death, but you deserve it,' the letter said. 'You will have electrodes connected to your shaved head and leg. You will be strapped into the electric chair and a mask will be placed over your face so they won't see it contort when you die. Two thousand volts will be sent through your body – they say the person's eyeballs sometimes explode, and sometimes flames erupt from the electrodes when the execution takes longer than expected. Wish we could be there to watch, Lucia, but only the victim's family is invited to watch. Shame.'

As a killing machine, it is not reliable. When John Evans went to the chair in 1983, flames erupted from the electrodes and his execution took fourteen minutes, after which he looked, said one doctor, 'like a barbecued chicken'.

Lucia wanted to die by firing squad. She was terrified of the chair, but in Alabama there is only the chair. She shuddered as she folded the letter and put it back in the envelope. There was something else inside, a newspaper cutting about the last woman to be executed in America: Versa Barfield, fifty-two, in 1984. When the killing began cheers erupted from pro-death marchers outside the prison.

Lucia's mother was pro-death and a member of a religious cult who believed all murderers should die. She hated her daughter's sin and from the moment she found about Nick Cohen's murder she believed the only way Lucia could save her soul was to repent and accept death as her punishment.

The real truth was that Lucia's mother was terrified of losing her daughter but more terrified of losing her husband, who was one of the most powerful leaders of the religious cult and had warned his wife to forget about Lucia or risk 'provoking the wrath of God'.

## SOMETHING TO REMIND YOU

It was all wrong but when Dan Kelly ordered his wife to send the letter and newspaper cutting to the prison she did not dare disobey and was so indoctrinated in any case that she had virtually convinced herself it was the right thing to do.

Lucia thought about suicide many times but it was virtually impossible to kill yourself in a place designed to keep inmates safe from harm, self-inflicted or otherwise.

And then the nightmares started. In them Nick Cohen was back from the dead and he walked Death Row. A grim apparition looking through the bars of every cell, searching for Lucia. He wanted revenge and she always woke screaming, believing he was really there.

In reality Nick Cohen was very dead and Lucia was glad, despite the terrible consequences. He had tried to strangle her because she refused sex, so she stabbed him. 'It was self-defence,' she told the court afterwards. 'He was going to kill me, I could tell by the look in his eyes that he wasn't going to stop. There was a knife by the bed, one I'd just used to eat dinner with. I grabbed it and stabbed him and he fell off the bed and staggered across the room and just sat down in a chair. Then he died.'

It was all too much for Lucia so she decided the only way she would ease her pain was to increase the amount of Thorazine she was taking and become a zombie. 'I figured that the more I took the less I would feel and that had to be better than going insane,' she said. 'The nightmares got worse and two of the guards were picking on me, and turned a blind eye when three other inmates sexually assaulted me. I had sent many letters to my son but they were not returned and I guess I had finally given up all hope. I wanted to die.'

But then one day Lucia received a letter. It was not from her son or mother. She had no idea who it was from. The sender was anonymous. Inside there was a pure silk bookmark with embroidered angels worshipping at the feet of Jesus and the words, 'He has risen, hallelujah. Love is stronger than death.'

'I was moved to tears,' she recalls. 'I don't know why because I was not a religious person. I guess I got sick of hearing about God when I was a child. My father was obsessed by good and evil, right and wrong and all that. I grew to hate it, really hate it.

'But there was something about the bookmark. The words touched me and I did something crazy. I sent it to my mother. Don't ask me why, I just did. It was an impulse thing.'

A month later she received a letter from her mother. It was the first of many and the correspondence continued for six months before a visit was arranged and her mother and son went to see her.

'I never thought it would happen. Even after I received a few letters from my mother and realised what was happening to her and why she had treated me so badly I did not hold out much hope of seeing her or my son.

'Then one day I got a letter from her explaining that she was planning to leave my father, who had been beating her. She had started to attend a Baptist church and accepted Jesus as her Saviour, all because of the bookmark.

'She could not stop thinking about the words 'love is stronger than death'. It had a profound effect on her. She told me that for the first time in her life she realised what Christianity was all about.

She said Jesus had changed her, made her realise that the religious cult she and her husband were part of was wrong. I could see she was different. Her eyes were full of life and I could feel love and compassion radiating from her. I knew I had to have what she had found.'

After several weeks studying the Bible and talking to the prison's spiritual adviser, Lucia became a Christian, accepting Jesus as her Saviour. Six months later, following an appeal, her sentence was unexpectedly reduced to life with the possibility of parole and she was allowed to see her son six times a year.

# 14

# View from above

*Burt Lyon, Detention Centre for Men, Dallas, Texas, USA*

'It's no big deal,' Burt says when asked how he became a Christian preacher. 'God works greater miracles every day and most of the time no one hears about them. What God did for me was marvellous, but the 'Big Fella' is awesome and you should never underestimate his power over sin. He loves a challenge, and my life was so messed up nothing short of a miracle would put it right.'

Burt first set eyes on Reverend John Kennedy six months before he tried to kill the priest with a deadly poisonous snake. Burt's mother, a deeply religious woman, wanted her only son to look up to the Reverend as some kind of father figure.

He had been a tower of strength when Burt's father walked out on his family. Burt was seventeen when it happened and the memory of the night when his father packed his bags and left his wife crying and begging him not to leave haunted him for a long time.

Burt first spoke to the Reverend when he was

praying for Burt's mother. It was only weeks after his father left and the Reverend stood in the kitchen of their home, on the outskirts of Dallas, Texas. Burt's mother sat in her cane chair. She was fifty but looked much older and frail.

Her eyes were red and sore and as the Reverend prayed Burt noticed her hands clasped tightly together trembling and holding a wet handkerchief. The Reverend's booming voice echoed around the room.

'For some reason it made me angry,' Burt recalls. 'My world had been torn apart and I was like a time bomb waiting to explode. My father walked out, leaving us all hurting real bad, and the bad thing for me was that he was a God-fearing man and had always taught me to believe in Christian values.

'When he left, for another woman, I wanted to kill him, but he'd disappeared and now this other man of God had turned up and I wanted to kill him too.'

The Reverend prayed and Burt stood outside the kitchen door and listened. His voice was loud and authoritative and the weight of the words gave the prayer substance, pouring it into the emptiness that had become their lives.

'Lord I pray in your mercy and compassion that you would take this precious life, this precious woman, into thy loving care,' the Reverend said, and he placed the palm of his hand on Burt's mother's head. 'Lord heal this broken heart,' he added.

The words seemed to hang in the air and after them a stillness descended like a soft blanket over the room.

## VIEW FROM ABOVE

Burt felt tears in his eyes and a strange warmth seeping into his body. He wanted to fight it, wanted to stand there unmoved, cold as a stone, but he could not so he kicked open the door and burst through the kitchen and out of the back door.

He wanted to run into the night until the pain in his chest exploded and his lungs burst and legs collapsed. He wanted to die, but remained rooted to the spot listening to the footsteps of the Reverend coming after him.

'Right then I wanted to die,' Burt remembers. 'I really wanted my life to be over. I wanted the night to swallow me, to take me into its blackness, through space and time to somewhere where nothing mattered and no one cared and where all the desperate lonely people vanished into nothing.

'But that was not going to happen and within seconds the Reverend with the big booming voice was striding across the back yard towards me. I think he wanted to help me but before he could say anything I punched him in the face and broke his nose.

'He went to the police and I was arrested which caused my mother to break down completely. He did not press charges and claimed he wanted to teach me a lesson. It was then I decided to kill him.'

Six weeks later Burt stood outside the door of the Reverend's ranch house. The red dust lifted and swirled in the breeze. The storm had passed and the sky began to lighten and the burnt-orange sun glared through the moving rain clouds and its warmth felt good.

Burt was pleased with himself. He'd just put a rattlesnake in the Reverend's front room and soon, he hoped, it would strike the Reverend dead.

Burt wiped the sweat from his brow and took a deep breath. He felt ill most of the time because he was drinking heavily, a bottle of whiskey every day, sometimes more, and taking drugs. He was sober now but still felt dizzy and staggered behind the house to where he had parked his car.

A few minutes later Burt saw the Reverend's jeep coming toward him about half a mile down the approach road to the ranch. 'Jesus, he's supposed to be out of town,' Burt said, but it was too late to hide and the Reverend looked at Burt as he drove past.

The Reverend wondered what Burt was doing near the ranch but a few moments after walking through his front door he found out. He was heading for the telephone after seeing Burt's tyre marks in the red dust, but stopped suddenly to find a rattlesnake spitting and rearing in front of him.

Its rattle was hideously loud and the way it thrashed about on the carpet sent fear cursing through the Reverend. For a moment he froze and the snake coiled and then darted forward striking with its venomous fangs. The Reverend clutched his leg and fell on to the snake. It struck again this time biting his face before moving quickly across the floor and under a cupboard.

'He should have been dead,' Burt said. 'The venom is fatal unless you receive the antidote immediately and the Reverend lay on the floor of his ranch house for several hours before God performed a miracle.

'No one knows for sure what exactly happened, but the Reverend says he started praying and then passed out but woke up feeling better than he did before the snake bit him. He shot it with a gun before calling the police and having me arrested again.

'My fingerprints were all over the ranch house and I ended up back in the same police cell only this time facing a charge of attempted murder.

'But then something happened, something so incredible that even now all these years later I find it hard to believe. I had a fit, some kind of epileptic seizure, right there in the police cell and I thought I was going to die.

'Later they told me it was the result of alcohol and drug abuse but at the time I thought I was having a heart attack. I felt a terrible sharp pain in my chest and head and fell over, banging my head on the wall before ended up flat out on the floor unable to move and choking on my own vomit. It was then I passed out.'

Incredibly, at the precise moment the Reverend was walking down the steps of the police building to where Burt was being detained. He had decided not to press charges and was planning to talk to Burt to see if he could help someone who appeared to be completely out of control and heading for disaster.

Now he wondered if he was too late. By the time they got the cell door open the Reverend feared Burt might be dead. He had stopped breathing and attempts to revive him were not working.

## GOSPEL BEHIND BARS

They called for a paramedic but the Reverend had other ideas. He placed his hand on Burt's head and in a loud voice said: 'In the name of Jesus live,' and suddenly Burt's eyes opened and he sat bolt upright coughing and spluttering.

'I was shocked,' Burt continued, recalling the moment he saw the Reverend standing over him. 'But not because of what I saw when I opened my eyes. Sure I did not expect to see the Reverend there; the police had not told me if he was alive or dead. They told me he'd had some kind of accident so obviously I figured the worst because by then I was starting to wish I had not done such a stupid thing.

'The thing that shocked me the most though was remembering what I had seen a few moments earlier. It sounds pretty strange but right there in that prison cell I had what can only be described as an out-of-body experience.

'I actually watched myself lying unconscious on the floor and saw the Reverend lay hands on me and bring me back to life. At the same time I was aware of a tremendous presence around me and realised that I was not the only one looking down on the scene.

'There were angels in the room, six or seven of them. They were watching over me and praising God as the Reverend prayed. And then, zap, I was back on the floor of the cell sitting up, kinda dazed and confused, trying to remember what had happened.'

The Reverend asked the police to leave him and Burt alone for a short while. Burt told him what had happened and the Reverend sat and listened and every few minutes whispered 'Amen, praise the Lord,' and then smiled and shook his head.

'You think I'm crazy, don't you?' Burt said.

'No, I think it's wonderful,' the Reverend replied, 'God's working a miracle in your life. If I was you I'd get on my knees and thank him, and then read this.'

The Reverend handed Burt a pocket New Testament Bible and stood up to leave.

'Wait, where are you going?' Burt said.

'Home. I've got a little cleaning up to do.'

Burt felt sick and held his head in his hands.

'Don't worry,' the Reverend said. 'I'm not going to press charges. It's forgotten and besides I believe something good is going to come out of all this. See you tomorrow.'

Burt read the Bible and prayed for several hours afterwards and for the first time in his life asked God for forgiveness. Immediately he felt a change come over him. The anger and the fear had gone, replaced by a peace and feeling of well-being that he had never experienced before.

He was released and spent the next six months studying the Bible and attending the Reverend's church. There he and his mother committed their lives to God and were baptised in the Holy Spirit.

Burt eventually went to a Christian ministry centre near Dallas where he trained as a missionary. He became the manager of a mission in Anchorage, Alaska, before returning to Texas to establish a mission for the homeless in Houston.

# 15

# Still life talking

*Larry Ogle, Tennessee Prison for Men, USA*

It was winter and the sky was filled with snow clouds, thick and heavy and still with the expectant hush of the coming storm, and Larry Ogle looked up past the razor-wire fences and guard towers and wondered if he would ever see snow fall on the farm where he used to live before he murdered his wife and son. He doubted it. The judge who sentenced him to life in jail said he would not be eligible for parole until his ninety-seventh birthday and Larry Ogle believed him. How many more winters in here? he thought. Fifty, maybe more. He closed his eyes and felt the first snow fall on his face. 'Oh God,' he whispered, 'please help me. I need your forgiveness.'

It was summer and the sun had been out and burning fiercely for some time when the police arrived at Larry's farm and began digging up the floor of the barn. The horse stalls had been covered in manure and lime to stop police dogs sniffing out the stench of the decomposing bodies, and the pungent smell leaked out and mingled with the odour of sweat as the men laboured in the heat.

Beneath the manure and lime, a foot down, they discovered the bodies of Larry's wife and son. The men gathered around the shallow grave and looked at the corpses. What was left of Liz and Dan Ogle just lay there black and crumpled and twisted in places where Larry had buried them three years earlier.

One of the men felt sick and walked out of the shade into the sun to get into the back of a white van. He pulled out two thick plastic body bags with zips up the front and stood for a moment while he breathed in the fresh air.

A post-mortem examination on Liz Ogle showed that she had suffered a brutal beating before she died. She had a broken neck, a shattered spine, and a broken rib. It was also discovered that her son Dan had been shot in the mouth and chest.

A few miles away Larry was stuffing a large amount of money into a plastic holdall, which he zipped shut and threw on to the bed of the trailer home where he had spent the past few days hiding.

He was planning to leave the country, maybe head down to Mexico or Brazil, but the next day the police got a tip-off that Ogle was hiding out at a trailer park and they found him cowering in the bathroom. The verdict was a foregone conclusion, so to avoid the death penalty Larry pleaded guilty and was sentenced to life in jail.

Larry Ogle, an ex-policeman turned farmer, was in his late forties when he killed his wife Liz, who

## STILL LIFE TALKING

was thirty-nine, and then a few months later when his twenty-one-year-old son Dan accused him of murder, Larry killed him as well.

Why? Because his honest, church-going wife and son found out that their formerly law-abiding husband and father had become a thief. Larry had turned into a common criminal to pay his bills, and became the murderer of two members of his own family to cover his tracks.

After Larry quit the police force he bought a farm and moved in with his wife, son and two daughters, Judy and Lynda, both in their late teens when Liz and Dan Ogle died. But after a few years as a farmer Larry found that he had trouble making ends meet so he began to steal tractors and other farm equipment.

Liz Ogle, a deeply religious woman, was shocked and pleaded with her husband to stop. He refused and they began arguing bitterly and she told him that she had reported him to the police and was planning to go to court to give evidence against him.

Weeks later Larry went to the police and reported that his wife had mysteriously disappeared. He claimed they had been having rows recently and she may have just left home. But the already suspicious police did not believe a word and thought he had killed Liz and disposed of the body.

Larry's daughter Judy told investigators that her mother was 'very frightened' of her husband in the weeks leading up to her disappearance and he became a prime suspect in a possible murder. The police carried out an extensive search of his farm but found nothing and Larry knew that without the discovery of a body there was no proof of murder in most cases.

Unable to convict Larry of murder, detectives stepped up the robbery case, hoping they could put him in jail even without his wife's testimony. When Larry's farmhouse was burnt down the police became further convinced that foul play was involved in Liz Ogle's disappearance. They believed that he was trying to destroy evidence – either of the murder or the theft of the farm equipment.

Eventually, the police felt they had enough evidence against Ogle for the theft of the farm equipment and he was arrested. What they did not count on was that Larry would be freed on bail until the trial a few months later. Within a matter of weeks police found Dan Ogle's truck abandoned two miles from his home. He was never seen alive again.

Larry's heartbroken son had been to the police before he also mysteriously vanished and said he believed his father had killed his mother. He wanted Larry arrested or at least interrogated by the murder squad.

Dan Ogle had also made several public statements which suggested that his father was responsible for his mother's death and these remarks led to a series of angry clashes with his father.

Police were now certain Larry had killed his son, but following another search of the farm they came up with nothing. As Larry had buried the bodies under horse manure and lime, the police dogs were not able to sniff out the stench of the decomposing bodies.

Larry went to court to stand trial on theft charges and was convicted and sentenced to four years in prison. As far as he was concerned he had got away with murder and would be paroled in a couple of years. His grisly secret was still hidden below the horse stalls of his barn.

But then it began. The flashbacks and the dreams and the guilt, words from scripture and the golden-edged pictures of Christ on the cross torn from the pages of his wife's Bible, her face radiant and smiling and weeping tears of blood wiped away by wings of angels and the tender caress of her son. Larry tossed and turned and the metal cell cot creaked with the motion of his fitful sleep while others listened.

Larry was not a religious man but he had never mocked his wife's faith. Towards the end when Liz Ogle had gone to church to pray for her husband he had sat at home flicking through the pages of a dog-eared Bible wondering if there was any truth in what his wife had told him about repentance and forgiveness. He thought of the story of Jesus who was the Son of God and had died on the cross so that men like Larry Ogle could be saved from themselves and hell.

He wished he had believed, but it was too late. Not only had he killed his wife and son but he was now telling people about it. Prison guards believed Larry was bragging to other inmates about murdering Liz and Dan but he was confessing his sin to ease the burning pain of guilt that raged like a fire in his mind and crushed his heart and soul with a force so powerful that there were times he thought he would just drop down dead.

Consumed by an overpowering fear of death and hell Larry told his Christian cellmate everything, even where his wife and son were buried. The fellow inmate went to the prison warden who contacted the police and they reopened the case by applying for a search warrant to dig up Larry's farm.

In the meantime Larry completed his sentence for the robberies and went home. For several weeks he thought about giving himself up. He knew the police were closing in and began to wish he had kept his mouth shut.

But the deep conviction that led to him to confess in prison was growing stronger. And the dreams and flashbacks, the words from scripture and visions of Christ, continued to trouble him until one night he woke up trembling with fear following a nightmare about hell: he stood in chains in complete darkness looking at heaven through a hole in the black sky.

On the other side he could see his wife and son happy and rejoicing in the company of angels. They could not see him and they could not hear his anguished screams as he tried to reach out and touch paradise. He shivered as he remembered the awful scene and realised that he could not run or hide from his own tormented soul and spirit.

'I could feel the hand of God on my life,' he later

recalled. 'There was no escape, none at all. It was if I no longer had any control over my actions. The guilt and conviction of God the Holy Spirit had already led me to own up to what I had done.

'Now I was rooted to the spot with the weight of sin in my life and I knew that I would end up back in prison convicted of murder. It was as though God was leading me to a place of repentance and forgiveness, a place where I would give what was left of my messed-up life to him.'

And that is exactly what happened to Larry. The police found what they were looking for, he was charged with the murders of his wife and son and sentenced to life in prison.

He was filled with such deep remorse and racked by such consuming guilt that during his first few months inside he became depressed and wanted to die. The only thing that stopped him was his new-found faith in God.

Then one day he was sitting in his cell and a preacher came by. He told Larry about the love of Jesus and the forgiveness of sin. He committed his life to God there and then and has been a regular member of the prison chapel congregation and Christian inmates' group ever since.

The warder of the prison admitted: 'Larry is a changed man. In all my years in the job I have seen many, many people "get religion" during their sentence, but never have I seen it have such a profound effect on an individual. Ogle obviously had some kind of divine experience. He looks as though he's got something the rest of us are striving for. Peace.'

# 16

# Back for good

*David Taylor, Lindholme Prison, Doncaster, England*

It was well after midnight on Christmas Eve. David, a forty-year-old former drug dealer, woke suddenly. Something was wrong, he could sense it: a presence around him in his dark prison cell. For a moment he just lay there looking at the ceiling and then it started to happen. A strange feeling. He knew he was not alone and he sat up quickly and looked around him. There was no one else there and yet the atmosphere was charged with a tremendous power and he trembled as he realised what was happening. The presence around him was divine. God the Holy Spirit was with him and David began to weep.

It was a miracle David survived at all to end up on his knees in a prison cell during the early hours of a cold winter morning asking Jesus to come into his life. Doctors said it was remarkable he was still alive after his mother was knocked down the stairs by his drunken father when she was eight months pregnant with him. And then years later David became an alcoholic and drug addict and risked premature death.

He had a bad start. The youngest of eleven children and born into a violent home by the sea in northeast England, David left school at fifteen and followed in his father's footsteps, becoming a deep sea fisherman and then a heavy drinker. It was not long before he ended up in trouble with the courts and then in prison.

It was a tough life at sea but David's drinking habits were over the top and he shocked other hardened fishermen with his potentially lethal cocktails of white spirit and after-shave lotion which he binged on before becoming extremely violent and increasingly unpredictable.

No one was really surprised when he was first sent to prison at the age of seventeen. 'He was a wild man, completely out of his mind most of the time,' a former workmate claimed some years later after David had joined the merchant navy.

He travelled the world and became involved in drugs, cannabis at first, but then LSD which made him so mentally ill he ended up seeing a psychiatrist. That did not put him off drugs and he progressed to selling them and, after getting into trouble with the authorities in Australia, he was arrested on his return to England and sent back to prison.

Later he got a good job in North Sea fire protection but while working abroad learnt that a friend had been raped. David was so angry when he found out that the police were not able to press charges that he took the law into his own hands, broke into the house of the alleged culprits and beat them up. He was given a suspended sentence.

After leaving his job in fire protection David bought a shop in Hull and made a good living selling furniture. But he became bored with the business and moved to Spain where he bought a yacht and was later caught planning a robbery, found guilty of conspiracy and returned to jail on a four-year sentence.

He found himself at a prison in the north of England, near Doncaster. He was depressed and considering taking drugs again when he ended up seeking refuge in the prison chapel during a riot.

It was the first time in his life that he had been in church. Some months later a former heroin addict came to the prison to talk about how Christianity had transformed his life. David was moved by the story. He knew what it was like to be dependent on drugs and was again smoking lots of dope (cannabis) which was widely available in prison.

The former addict's story, though, inspired David to investigate the Bible and for the first time he began to question the meaning of life.

'I began to understand what a vain, conceited and selfish person I was,' he recalled. 'I started to think about all the terrible things I had done in my life, all the mistakes and the pain and suffering. I hated what I had become and wanted to change. Deep inside something was happening to me, something I could not explain.

'Then on Christmas Eve I woke up in the early

hours of the morning and felt a tremendous presence around me and I knew at that precise moment that Jesus had died for me. I simply said I was sorry and really meant it and asked Jesus to come into my life.

'The old life just flooded out of me and when I awoke the next day I was a brand new person. The Bible says the truth will set you free and that was my experience. I was extremely happy but there was a lot of cynicism. People doubted, and who could blame them?

'But I realised that Jesus was the way, the truth, and the life and that there was no life without him. God had transformed me. It was a dramatic conversion, a miracle, and I guess I would not have believed it possible had it not happened to me.'

David was eventually released from prison after successfully studying the Bible by correspondence and several years later graduated from university with an honours degree in applied science. He eventually returned to prison to work as a chaplain.

# 17

# It don't lie

*Sally-Anne McKenzie-Paine, Miami Detention Centre for Women, USA*

It was a chance meeting. Fate maybe. She was desperate. He had the answer. God. It was that simple. Black and white, life and death, yes or no. She said yes and lived; born-again. Had she said no, well this story would probably not be worth telling. It sounds heartless, but who wants to hear about another junkie death. Period.

It all started to go wrong for Sally-Anne when she went to America in the early 1970s. A haze of cannabis-induced highs led to a bad 'trip' after taking LSD and suddenly Sally-Anne's previously steady and secure world became a rocky world.

The well-educated and well-grounded girl from the comfortable upper-class home life, with holidays abroad and doting parents, had climbed aboard a mind-altering emotional roller-coaster ride to hell with no stop signs.

Back home in England Sally-Anne began training as a classical jazz dancer. It was a kind of 'fix', not the same as being stoned in the States, but she was sure that the dance-drug would solve her emotional problems. She was wrong. And then came heroin, readily available and relatively cheap on the streets of Paris where she was working with a jazz company. Soon she was heavily addicted.

In 1978 Sally-Anne moved back to London where she planned to get help. But her father died and then she lost her first baby. Instead of coming off heroin she started to rely more and more heavily on it. 'The more I took, the more terrified I became of what I was doing so I ended up taking even more,' she admitted years later. 'I was high most of the time and eventually became a recluse.'

At the end of the summer of 1980 Sally-Anne collapsed at her mother's house and was forced to seek treatment for her addiction. She booked into a rehabilitation clinic and eventually came off heroin completely. 'I should have been the happiest person alive,' she said, 'but on leaving the clinic I experienced a feeling of intense loss and terrible depression. They warned me I might feel down but I never expected it to hit me so hard.'

So in a fit of desperation Sally-Anne returned to America. She had friends in Miami and needed their help. It was a bad move. Within months she was back on drugs. This time it was cocaine and once again her world started falling apart. She was soon asked to leave her friends' home and ended up living on the streets using cocaine through a needle. Eventually she was picked up by the police and sent

# IT DON'T LIE

to a detention centre for women.

Sally-Anne had hit rock bottom. She was ashamed and depressed and desperate. Then one day she was sitting in her cell and a preacher came by. Something about him impressed her. 'I was racked by a consuming guilt and he told me about the love of Jesus and the forgiveness of sins,' she recalls.

'My heart was moved in a new way and for the first time ever I saw light at the end of this dark tunnel. I committed my life to God there and then and asked Jesus to come in and be my Lord and Saviour.'

Twenty-four hours later Sally-Anne was miraculously released from prison and returned to England once again. She has never used drugs since. In 1989 she went to live with her mother in South Africa, completed a Licentiate in Christian Ministry and has since worked as a missionary among the black people of KaNgwane.

# 18

# In the end

*Anonymous*

He could remember now, clearly and vividly, and tears formed in the corner of his eyes as he saw his mother and heard her voice and smelled the delicate fragrance of her perfume as she held him tightly in her arms and kissed him goodnight. Then she was gone and he shut his eyes tightly to try to bring her back but there was only darkness now and he held his head in his hands and rocked back and forth on the edge of the prison bunk. He wished she was here to hold him now. Just for a moment, just one last goodnight kiss before he went to sleep for ever. 'Heavenly Father,' he whispered, 'I'm scared. I feel so scared and alone, please help me.'

Lee first spoke to the prison chaplain two years after arriving on Death Row. It was the first time in his life that Lee had asked about God. He had never been to church, prayed, or read the Bible, not even during his childhood. Not that he had much of a childhood. He had been on drugs since he was ten and on the wrong side of the law ever since.

But now he was desperate. He was thirty-four and knew he probably would not live to see his fortieth birthday. 'They are going to execute me,' he told the chaplain during their first meeting. 'I probably deserve to die anyway, but I want to make my peace with God before I go. Show me how, please.'

'What is your name?' asked the chaplain.

'Lee,' came the reply.

'Do you believe in God?'

'Yes sir I do now,' Lee said. 'I never used to but I've had a lot of time to think lately and I don't want to go to hell.'

The chaplain sat down on the edge of bunk next to Lee and thought for a moment. 'It's not a quick fix,' he said. 'God loves you Lee and I am prepared to lead you through a prayer of repentance and confession of faith, but unless you really mean it, we would both be wasting our time. Do you understand what I am saying?'

Lee nodded. He had tears in his eyes and reached out a hand. 'Please,' he said taking hold of the chaplain's wrist. 'I have no peace in my life. I have led a bad life and hurt a lot of people and I will pay the ultimate price for my crimes, but right now I don't want to live another minute without knowing God's forgiveness. Please help me.'

The chaplain nodded and placed his hand on Lee's head and prayed over him. Lee made a commitment to Christ and experienced a filling by the Holy Spirit which caused him to faint. He slept for seven hours and when he woke up and looked in the mirror he

# IN THE END

barely recognised himself. 'There is something very different about you today,' a prison guard said.

'I've got God,' Lee replied.

'Good, you're going to need him,' and the guard laughed as he walked away to check the other cells.

Lee had been in prison twice before for robbery. The second time he got nine years but served only five. He killed a young man and woman eight months later. They were in their mid-twenties and worked in the shop that Lee decided to rob. Neither of them stood a chance because Lee had already made up his mind to leave no witnesses.

He put a gun behind the ear of the woman and shot her before shooting the man in the face. Then he stole $70,000 of jewellery but was arrested less than a week later after police caught a man who had helped Lee to plan the robbery. The detective who led the investigation said it was the most brutal cold-blooded killing he had ever seen. 'There was no argument; he just blew their brains out,' he said.

Lee signed a confession and led police to the gun, but pleaded not guilty to try and avoid the death penalty. The trial lasted two and a half weeks. The jury found him guilty and Lee was sentenced to death.

He was taken to Death Row and, following several unsuccessful appeals during a five-year period, the courts decided he would stay on Death Row and the judge eventually gave Lee the execution date. He was to be executed by lethal injection within six months.

Lee could see the victim's family behind the

window of the execution chamber. He had been prepared. His limbs were strapped down and he had the injection tube in his arm. He had a clean white uniform. The executioners were hidden behind a two-way mirror. The chaplain stood next to Lee.

'Thank you,' Lee whispered and smiled at the chaplain, then made his statement.

He said: 'I believe Jesus Christ is my Saviour and I'm sorry.'

The chaplain nodded and closed his eyes.

Lee looked up, took a deep breath and said: 'I'm ready.'

His body rose and he gasped as his lungs relaxed, expelling the air. There was no pain. Then he was dead.

'I have seen God at work in men and women in prison many times,' the chaplain said afterwards. 'But I was taken by surprise by the change in Lee during his last few years on Death Row. He was given an opportunity to accept Christ and he grasped it with all his heart and soul. I have not seen many people respond so readily to the Christian message as Lee did. In the end he found a way back into the heart of God. He knew that while people would never forgive him for taking those two innocent lives, God would and God alone can save a person's soul.'

# 19

# Prophecy

*Anonymous*

The evening sun, hidden in a storm sky, lightened the edge of the low clouds burnt orange and red in places where the descending darkness touched. Distant thunder rumbled and David felt the first drops of rain. His face was already wet with tears and he looked up at the changing sky. He gazed out across fields and forest, a vast patchwork tract of countryside, stretching out from the foot of the hill he had climbed.

He now stood at the top, as high as he could go, balanced astride a rock like some great mountaineer filling his lungs with the sweet conquest of altitude. David felt good. He had climbed the hill to celebrate his freedom. Freedom from prison, freedom from heroin. 'I'm free,' he bellowed. 'I'm free. Thank you God, thank you,' and he jumped up and down and shouted for joy.

Four months earlier David was suicidal. A heroin addict, he had assaulted his wife and set fire to the house and ended up in prison. He had wanted to die until a chaplain went to see him in a strip-cell, the place where suicidal inmates are held, for their own safety.

David was going out of his mind and the strip-cell made him worse. He had tried to kill himself twice and almost succeeded, but now he was helpless. They had taken away his last chance to escape the pain and torment of a life which had become unbearable.

In a fit of depression he cried: 'How do you get God? I need Him.'

The chaplain told him and David immediately made a commitment to Christ and experienced a filling with the Holy Spirit. Within a week he was such a different person that the prison warder allowed him to be moved from the strip-cell and back into a normal cell in the main part of the prison.

'He came to Christ and the experience had a profound effect on him,' the chaplain said. 'So much so that he began to clean himself up. On visiting David, his wife said, "What's different about you?" She could not believe it.'

The night before David went to court, the prison Bible study group prayed for him. Someone shared a prophecy which simply said, 'Go home'. The next day, David was given two years' probation. He is now training to become a church leader.

# 20

# Bitterness rising

*Chan Hopthui, Exeter Prison, Devon, England*

The young man wears a dirty white vest tucked into a pair of torn jeans. He is a little pale and shaky, the way convalescents are. His left arm he carries crooked and low and some of his fingers are missing. His flesh is scarred in places where it has been badly burned and tattooed in other places and the puncture marks from hypodermic injections are clearly visible.

He says he is thirty but looks twice as old and you can tell he is in pain by the way he moves. He is a shell of a man, fragile and damaged and wasted. He sits down at a table in the room where other recovering drug addicts wait for counselling and with his good arm points to where an older man is seated, arms outstretched, across a table to hold hands with a distraught expectant mother who has passed on her heroin addiction to her unborn baby.

'He gives us all hope,' the young man says. 'His name is Mr Chan and before God saved him to help people like me he was an evil man whom many people wanted dead.'

## GOSPEL BEHIND BARS

Mr Chan was a member of the vicious Triad Chinese Mafia, the same Mafia who had supplied the young man with heroin and then cut off his fingers and burned his skin with a blow torch when he could not afford to pay for his drug addiction.

Mr Chan was feared in the criminal underworld of the Far East, where the consequences of his trade left a trail of death and destruction, until one day a chance meeting in an English prison changed his life and ultimately the lives of those he used to hurt to get rich.

He was serving a long sentence for smuggling heroin into Britain when he turned to Christianity after reading of the conversion of a woman he once despised for ruining his life. She was an Englishwoman who was arrested in Bangkok in 1977 for heroin smuggling, but always protested she was tricked into carrying drugs for her Hong Kong Chinese boyfriend.

Mr Chan, who was from Malaysia but did much of his business in Thailand, was staying in the hotel next door to hers at the time and the case aroused international interest and led to a tightening of security at customs checks in the region.

He was forced to lie low and his wealth eventually ran out, forcing him to take even greater risks in a desperate attempt to rebuild his collapsed drugs empire. He was already drinking heavily and suffering from depression and paranoia when his world finally fell apart completely when he was caught and convicted of smuggling heroin.

## BITTERNESS RISING

Mr Chan was full of contempt for the Englishwoman arrested in Bangkok and blamed her for the fact that he was now in a similar situation as a foreigner in prison thousands of miles from home. He was lonely, depressed and desperately homesick, and the growing remorse for the mess he had made of his life and the pain inflicted on his wife and four children was eating away inside him like some kind of cancer. So as a last resort he prayed to God for help.

'I need a miracle,' he begged.

The answer came while he was sharing a cell with a Christian inmate during a snowstorm in the south of England. Mr Chan was in transit from one prison to another, but bad weather meant a week-long stop at another jail where the born-again prisoner told him how Jesus had changed his life.

Mr Chan had been wondering for some time whether the 'Christian God' could help him and now, stuck in a filthy, cold cell and contemplating the murder of another inmate who was tormenting him, he rummaged through the drawers for something to read.

He found a Bible with most of its pages missing and another dog-eared book with no cover. It did not look too promising but the title of the opening chapter – 'Bangkok' – aroused his interest. So he put the loose pages back in order and began to read.

The story seemed strangely familiar and, then, to his amazement, he discovered it was all about the English nurse who had caused him all that trouble.

But her awful experiences in the notorious Lard Yao women's prison, near which he used to live, won his sympathy. Like him, she too began to wonder about God until she was converted to Christ after speaking to a missionary visiting the prison.

Mr Chan finished the book in tears and next day during exercise hour asked his born-again fellow-inmate how he too could become a Christian. Back in his cell he fell to his knees acknowledging that Jesus was the God whom he sought and was overwhelmed by joy and peace.

He asked God to forgive him and the violent former Chinese Mafia boss, who only days before was planning to kill another prisoner, was soon a changed man. 'I realised Christ had taken the punishment I deserved by dying in my place on the cross,' he said. 'In time I was able to forgive others and for the first time in my life resist the temptation to become involved in violence.

'The change which came over me was amazing,' he added, 'I knew God had saved me, I felt it deep in my soul. I had peace within me, a wonderful, wonderful peace. It was the miracle I had asked for.'

Mr Chan dedicated the rest of his prison sentence to studying the Bible. He completed several Bible correspondence courses, attended Bible studies and prayer meetings. 'I developed a hunger for the things of God,' he said. 'I realised it was too late to do anything about the consequences of my past life, which resulted in death and destruction, but I asked forgiveness of all those I had hurt, especially my family.

## BITTERNESS RISING

'I explained to them what God had done in my life and both my son and daughter also became Christians. They saw what God was doing in my life and wanted the same joy and peace in their own lives.'

Mr Chan's release and subsequent deportation in 1989 was overshadowed by tough new anti-drug laws in Malaysia and the death penalty could not be ruled out, despite the completion of his prison sentence in Britain.

He was arrested on arrival in Malaysia but he was set free after fifty days in detention. Immediately he set about establishing a drug rehabilitation centre, incredibly helping those who only years before he may have had killed for the Triad Chinese Mafia.